NORTH SEA OIL

RESOURCE REQUIREMENTS FOR DEVELOPMENT
OF THE U.K. SECTOR

NORTH SEA OIL

RESOURCE REQUIREMENTS FOR DEVELOPMENT OF THE U.K. SECTOR

J. Kenneth Klitz

PERGAMON PRESS

OXFORD · NEW YORK · TORONTO · SYDNEY · PARIS · FRANKFURT

U.K.	Pergamon Press Ltd., Headington Hill Hall, Oxford OX3 0BW, England
U.S.A.	Pergamon Press Inc., Maxwell House, Fairview Park, Elmsford, New York 10523, U.S.A.
CANADA	Pergamon of Canada, Suite 104, 150 Consumers Road, Willowdale, Ontario M2J 1P9, Canada
AUSTRALIA	Pergamon Press (Aust.) Pty. Ltd., P.O. Box 544, Potts Point, N.S.W. 2011, Australia
FRANCE	Pergamon Press SARL, 24 rue des Ecoles, 75240 Paris, Cedex 05, France
FEDERAL REPUBLIC OF GERMANY	Pergamon Press GmbH, 6242 Kronberg-Taunus, Hammerweg 6, Federal Republic of Germany

The opinions expressed in this book are those of the author, and are not necessarily those of IIASA or the National Member Organizations that support it.

First edition 1980

British Library Cataloguing in Publication Data

Klitz, J Kenneth
North Sea oil.
1. Offshore oil industry - North Sea
2. Petroleum in submerged lands - North Sea
I. Title   II. International Institute for
Applied Systems Analysis
333.8'2   HD9575.N57   79-41017
ISBN 0 08 024442 4

Typeset by the International Institute for Applied Systems Analysis, Laxenburg, Austria, and printed by Novographic, Vienna, Austria

Dedicated to

SHANLEY

CONTENTS

FOREWORD

As part of a continuing program of research into energy resources and strategies, the WELMM (Water, Energy, Land, Manpower, and Materials) approach has been developed at IIASA to provide a better understanding of the systems aspects of energy-resource exploitation and its interaction with the other main natural and human resources. A major part of any WELMM assessment is the collection of data, which are either widely spread through the available literature (generally resulting in a lack of coherence and consistency) or, even worse, not published or not initially intended for publication. After the data have been gathered, checked, and made internally consistent, it is then possible to make more accurate comparisons of the resources required for various related schemes and to aggregate the data to show the overall requirements for any particular phase or project.

This book describes the results of a WELMM regional case study of North Sea oil discovery and production. From a technological point of view the development of the North Sea oil and gas fields is particularly interesting. It is a relatively recent and continuing process and it has several notable "frontier" aspects: production and exploration drilling are being carried out in deeper waters than ever before and this, in conjunction with the very difficult weather conditions in the area, has led to new design concepts for the steel or concrete platforms employed.

It is hoped that the large number of data collected here will demonstrate the interest of the WELMM approach and will be useful for future studies of energy strategies which rely on offshore oil and gas.

Michel Grenon
Task Leader
IIASA Resources Group

PREFACE

This book presents the results of a study of the quantities of natural and human resources needed to develop the oil fields currently considered commercially viable in the U.K. sector of the North Sea. Using the WELMM approach developed at IIASA, the study attempts to investigate and quantify the amounts of water, energy, land, manpower, and materials required to construct and operate the different facilities in use in the fields or planned for future installation. Starting from this detailed information on each facility the data are aggregated to show the total amount of resources needed to develop first each field and then the entire U.K. sector. Further, the study shows where and when resources are expended during the development of an offshore field and provides a quantitative comparison of the resource requirements for the various stages of development.

Because the study gives detailed information on most of the facilities typically required to develop an offshore field, it is hoped that the results will be useful for extrapolation to other North Sea fields as they become commercially viable and to offshore fields in other parts of the world where water depths and climatic conditions are similar. The North Sea case study is one of a series of IIASA studies which are investigating the resources needed to develop and operate a number of different energy-supply options (including North Sea oil, oil shales, enhanced oil recovery, coal, and nuclear energy); work continues on comparisons between the resource requirements of these various supply strategies.

The collection and aggregation of data formed the major parts of the study. A series of 509 questions per field was drawn up to obtain the necessary information and the answers were obtained in a number of ways: by an extensive search through the available literature, including industrial and oil-trade publications, from personal knowledge and contacts with colleagues working in related areas, and, in large part, through considerable cooperation with the oil companies involved in the North Sea.

It must be emphasized that not all resource requirements have been included in the subsequent tables, charts, and figures: in this sense the book underestimates the total effort required to develop the oil fields of the North Sea. An attempt has been made to capture the essential elements of the total effort in the U.K. sector, but where data were unavailable or quantities of materials were considered negligible, they were simply not included. It should also be understood that the study included all facilities needed to produce the crude oil and deliver it either to tankers or to the onshore terminals, but that the tankers, onshore terminals (at Sullom Voe, Flotta, and Cruden Bay), and onshore pipelines themselves were not included. It is anticipated that other studies, presently underway, will provide similar data about the offshore oil fields of the Norwegian sector and the U.K.-sector gas fields. Taken together, these studies will provide a more complete survey of the total effort being expended to obtain oil and gas from the North Sea.

I would like to express my appreciation to Professor Michel Grenon of IIASA for his suggestions, guidance, and criticisms; to the many operating oil companies and other organizations involved in the North Sea who readily supplied the data required and reviewed earlier drafts with comments and notations of errors; to Tim Devenport who carried out the large task of editing this book; to the International Business Machines Corporation (IBM) for making my time available for the study; to Dr. Roy M. Knapp of the University of Oklahoma, Norman, Okla., for a careful review; and to Dr. Robert J. Peckham of the Joint Research Centre, Commission of the European Communities, Ispra, Italy for his cooperation and assistance. This study was undertaken as part of the WELMM project at IIASA, supported, in part, by the United Nations Environment Programme (UNEP).

UNITS AND CONVERSION FACTORS

An attempt has been made to use SI or SI-derived units wherever possible in the text. Thus, for example, energies are given in joules (J), land areas in square kilometers (km^2), and weights in metric tonnes (tonne). However, in a number of cases the less-systematic U.S. and Imperial units are still in widespread use so that, for example, pipeline diameters are quoted in inches (in.) and some subsidiary calculations of distances and areas are performed in miles and acres, respectively. Direct conversions to SI or SI-derived units are given wherever appropriate.

Because the quantities of energy involved are usually large, they are normally expressed in billions of joules, for which the SI abbreviation is GJ (GJ = *giga*joule = 10^5 joules). One GJ is approximately equal to 278 kilowatt-hours, 72 pounds of coal, 6.8 U.S. gallons of oil, or 920 standard cubic feet of natural gas. All electrical energy is measured in joules electric (Je); wherever electrical energy is combined with fuel energy or included in energy totals it is assumed that the electricity is produced by a power plant of 33% fuel-to-electricity conversion efficiency. In these cases Je values are multiplied by 3 before inclusion in J-value totals.

A list of the more important conversion factors is given overleaf.

LIST OF CONVERSION FACTORS Values are given exactly or to a maximum of three significant figures. The standard prefixes k (= kilo = $\times 10^3$), M (= mega = $\times 10^6$), and G (= giga = $\times 10^9$) are used to indicate multiples of basic units.

to convert	into	multiply by
pound (avoirdupois)	kg	4.536×10^{-1}
ton (short, U.S.)	tonne (metric = 1000 kg)	9.072×10^{-1}
ton (short, U.S.)	pound (avoirdupois)	2.000×10^3
ton (long, U.K.)	pound (avoirdupois)	2.240×10^3
inch	m	2.540×10^{-2}
foot	m	3.048×10^{-1}
mile (statute)	km	1.609×10^0
m	foot	3.281×10^0
km	mile (statute)	6.214×10^{-1}
acre	km^2	4.047×10^{-3}
foot^3	m^3	2.832×10^{-2}
yard^3	m^3	7.646×10^{-1}
m^3	foot^3	3.531×10^1
tonne crude oil	barrel (U.S.)	7.340×10^0
barrel (U.S.) crude oil	tonne	1.362×10^{-1}
gallon (U.S.) crude oil	tonne	3.250×10^{-3}
gallon (U.S.)	m^3	3.785×10^{-3}
J (joule)	kcal (kilocalorie)	2.388×10^{-4}
J	kWh (kilowatt-hour)	2.777×10^{-7}
J	Btu (British thermal unit)	9.477×10^{-4}
GJ	kcal	2.388×10^{5}
GJ	kWh	2.777×10^2
GJ	Btu	9.477×10^5
kcal	J	4.187×10^3
kcal	GJ	4.187×10^{-6}
kcal	Btu	3.968×10^0
kWh	J	3.600×10^6
kWh	GJ	3.600×10^{-3}
kWh	Btu	3.413×10^3
Btu	J	1.054×10^3
Btu	GJ	1.054×10^{-6}
Btu	kcal	2.520×10^{-1}
Btu	kWh	2.930×10^{-4}
h.p. (horsepower, U.S.)	Js (joule-second)	7.457×10^2
tonne fuel oil	kWh	$\sim 1.455 \times 10^4$
tonne fuel oil	GJ	$\sim 5.238 \times 10^1$
barrel (U.S.) fuel oil	kcal	$\sim 1.585 \times 10^6$

1 INTRODUCTION

The North Sea lies in a sedimentary basin laid down during the Carboniferous, Jurassic, and Tertiary periods, which occurred between 350 million and 2 million years ago. During and since these periods, the appropriate strata for the formation of petroleum and natural gas have developed in the area.

During 1959, a large onshore discovery of natural gas was made at Slochteren in the Groningen province of the Netherlands, and it was thought likely that structures similar to the Slochteren field extended offshore in a northerly direction. Agreement of territorial rights of the countries adjacent to the North Sea was reached in the early 1960s and ratified by the United Kingdom in 1964. Upon ratification, exploration drilling was begun.

The first discovery of hydrocarbons in the North Sea was the West Sole gas field which was found by BP in 1965. Production started in 1967 and the gas was transported by pipeline to Easington in northeast England. In 1966 the three large gas fields, Hewett, Leman Bank, and Indefatigable were discovered off the Norfolk coast. In subsequent years additional gas finds were made in the southern sections of the North Sea.

The first North Sea oil was discovered in the Danish sector in 1966 but was not of commercial value. The Ekofisk oil field, located in Norwegian waters, was the first major oil discovery, and it resulted in the subsequent large-scale activities of exploration and discovery of oil fields in the North Sea.

In the U.K. sector the first oil find was made by the British Gas Corporation/Amoco group with their Montrose field, which was discovered in December 1969 but not announced as commercially exploitable until four years later. BP discovered the Forties field in November 1970 and announced its commercial viability in December 1971. As of July 1980, there are 14 fields producing oil in the U.K. sector, and an additional 11 fields are under development. Figure 1.1 illustrates the 23 oil fields studied here and the locations of various onshore terminals and platform-fabrication sites.

All the oil fields of the North Sea are located in the northern and middle parts of the area. The fields have been arranged or classified into the following groups:

(a) The southern group (east of England), including Argyll, Auk, and Fulmar
(b) The Aberdeen—Orkney group (east of Scotland), including Forties, Piper, Beryl A, Claymore, Montrose, Tartan, Maureen, Buchan, Brae, and Beatrice
(c) The east of Shetland group, including Brent, Thistle, Dunlin, North and South

FIGURE 1.1 The middle and northern parts of the U.K. sector of the North Sea, showing the 23 oil fields studied, the sites of some important onshore facilities, and the intersectoral boundaries.

Cormorant, Heather, Statfjord, Ninian, Magnus, Murchison, North West Hutton, and Hutton

The North Sea has become a major source of petroleum largely because of the size of the estimated recoverable reserves and the exceptionally high production rates in the fields. The remaining recoverable reserves on the U.K. continental shelf have been estimated, by the U.K. Department of Energy, as of June, 1980, to be in the range of 2000–4400 million tonnes (15,000–33,000 million barrels).

In the United Kingdom, government policy has been to promote rapid development of North Sea resources to eliminate dependence on imported energy. The amount of oil produced in the U.K. sector is expected to be 1.8–1.9 million barrels per day by the end of 1980, thus making the U.K. self-sufficient in oil. After this date, the annual U.K. production is expected to be between 95 and 135 million tonnes (700–1000 million barrels) per year. However, there are still uncertainties as to total production of petroleum from the North Sea over the next twenty or thirty years. Much remains to be determined regarding the recovery percentages and rates, future discoveries, and the development of the smaller fields already discovered.

THE WELMM APPROACH

The development of energy resources requires progressively more and more natural and/or human resources. This is due mainly to the increasing difficulty in "harvesting" primary energy resources and the increasing complexity of processes necessary to convert primary energy into final usable energy. It is apparent that we are entering a period of additional constraints and higher costs in the production of energy, basic materials, and commercial water, and in securing land. Consequently, this in turn is affecting the transformation of natural resources into the processed resources that are consumed in the economic system (see Figure 1.2). The major factors responsible are:

- The necessity to exploit less easily obtainable resources
- The increase in process requirements due to the necessity of using resources of decreasing quality
- Increased environmental constraints

As the resource-production system becomes more important, and the constraints increase, one cannot analyze each resource or resource-processing system independently. On the contrary, the analysis must be performed within a global framework, integrating all the qualitative and quantitative interrelations of the natural resources.

It is within this context that the WELMM approach has been developed as a means of analyzing the complex resource problem. The WELMM approach is an impact-matrix concept and mainly focuses on five limited resources: Water, Energy, Land, Manpower, and Materials. The basic objective is to assess the natural resource requirements of resource-development strategies (especially energy strategies) within specific countries or regions, or at the global level.

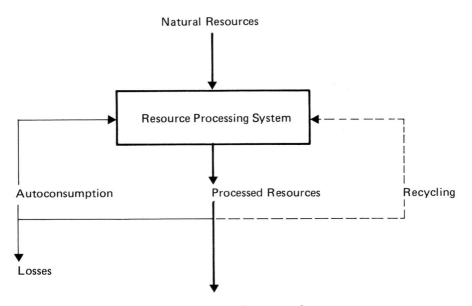

Natural Resources

Resource Processing System

Autoconsumption   Processed Resources   Recycling

Losses

Resources Available for the Economic System

Resource   the production factors mobilized in a production process,
                                  or more generally in an economic activity, e.g. capital,
                                  manpower, energy, water, . . .

Natural (or Primary) Resources   the resources available in the natural environment: solar
                                  energy, coal, uranium ore, water, non-energy minerals
                                  (bauxite, iron ore), wood, . . . For mineral resources, this
                                  includes the economic-geologic classification of resource
                                  base, resources and reserves

Processed (or Final) Resources   natural resources after transformation or upgrading (ex-
                                  traction or collection, processing, transportation, distri-
                                  bution, and possibly storage) to the condition in which
                                  they are consumed by the final user, e.g. final energy
                                  commodities, tap drinking water, basic materials such as
                                  steel, aluminum, glass, cement

Resource Processing System   a set of technological chains describing the linked series
                                  of activities necessary to make natural resources available
                                  to the final consumer (industries, households, . . .).

FIGURE 1.2 Natural resource cycle (basic definitions).

4

This is not a substitute for classical economic analysis, but rather a complement to it, allowing for a more detailed study. Also, when long-term economic projections are considered unreliable, the WELMM approach can be used as a first assessment of natural-resource requirements. In addition, it should be stressed that the WELMM approach is technology oriented and not time dependent. The resources necessary to implement a particular energy strategy are dependent on the technology employed and not on the time when implemented. The WELMM approach also attempts to emphasize constraints on resources that might not otherwise be indicated by a purely monetary evaluation.

The WELMM requirements are those natural or processed resources (Figure 1.2) necessary to construct or produce a particular process facility* and then to operate the same facility over some time period (Figure 1.3).

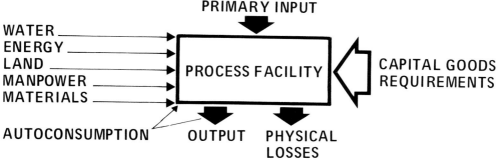

FIGURE 1.3 Process analysis.

The total WELMM requirements for either the construction or operation of facilities are composed of a subset of requirements, which are classified as direct, indirect, or capital (Figure 1.4). The reason for distinguishing between direct and indirect requirements is to allow for ease of calculation and manipulation of data. The direct requirements are those readily identified as being necessary to produce a particular facility or project and whose quantities are unique to each project or study. In contrast, the indirect requirements are those resources needed to produce, e.g., one tonne of steel or aluminum, and such requirements are generally consistent from one project to another. Hence, once the calculations for indirect resource requirements have been made and computerized they can be utilized throughout the various WELMM studies. For example, a study that evaluates and compiles all the direct requirements might include a compilation of all the steel needed to construct a pipeline, the energy required to weld the pipe, and the fuels needed to operate the offshore pipeline-laying barge. A complementary study of indirect requirements would extend the analysis to show the indirect water, materials, land, and manpower necessary to produce the steel found in the steel pipeline, to produce the welding rod, or to refine the fuels that operate the pipeline-laying barge. In the next chapter, Table 2.1 provides a detailed description of what is included in the direct and indirect categories for the North Sea study.

---

*A facility is any device that is constructed to handle or process resources, and/or to control the processing of resources. A facility performs one or more processes.

5

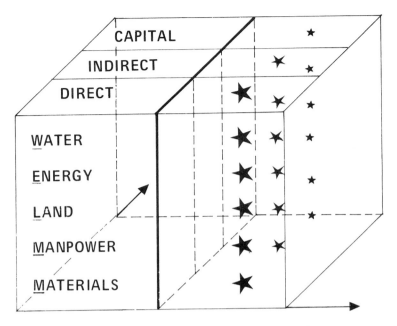

FIGURE 1.4 WELMM requirements to construct and/or to operate a facility.

The capital WELMM requirements refer to those that are necessary to generate major pieces of capital equipment that are employed for a period of time in the construction or operation of a facility. Such capital equipment is of general purpose and can serve other facilities as required; examples include lay barges, tugs, and derrick barges.

A more detailed explanation of the WELMM technique is provided in the IIASA Research Report "The WELMM Approach to Energy Strategies and Options" [1].

6

2 RESOURCE REQUIREMENTS FOR DEVELOPMENT OF THE U.K. SECTOR

This chapter summarizes the total direct resource requirements necessary to develop those fields in the U.K. sector of the North Sea that are currently considered to be commercially viable. The expenditure of resources for such development began with the first marine seismic surveys in 1966, and will continue until the mid-1980s when the last production wells are drilled. This chapter attempts to show the quantities of resources necessary for the *total* development of these U.K. fields, and also for each particular development *phase* over the same period.

The terms "direct" and "indirect" resources have been briefly discussed in Chapter 1, but because these two definitions are quite important in understanding what has been included or excluded in the subsequent tables and figures, they will be expanded upon here. To help the reader's understanding of the two terms, Table 2.1 shows examples of those resources included in each category for the North Sea study. The lists in the table are not comprehensive but hopefully they provide the necessary insight to understand the two definitions.

The data summarized in this chapter are derived from two sources: (1) data supplied by the operating companies, describing their specific and unique facilities, and (2) base data provided for typical facilities and given in Chapter 6. Examples of type (1) data include unique facilities such as platform substructure, deck, modules, and piles driven. Type (2) data include such items as field pipelines, gas vents, and exploration and production wells, where the facility is not necessarily unique.

FIELD DEVELOPMENT

The process of finding oil in the North Sea and developing the technology required to produce it and transport it to shore is a major and complex task, given the hostile environment. 858 offshore exploration and appraisal wells have been drilled in the U.K. sector to date, but only 144 can be allocated to the 23 fields covered in this study*.

---

*In this report, 23 of the 25 U.K. oil fields at various stages of development have been studied. Since this work is an evaluation of the U.K. sector, the Statfjord field, which lies on the border of the U.K. and Norwegian sectors, was not included in the analyses. The Heather field was also excluded, in this case because of the lack of available in-depth data. However, the Murchison field has been included in the analyses, because the major part of the field lies within the U.K. sector and only a small part overlaps the border of the Norwegian sector.

TABLE 2.1 Qualitative description[a] of resource requirements included as "direct" or excluded and therefore "indirect".

Resource	Direct requirements	Indirect requirements
Water	Water used at sites of platform and pipeline construction, and pipeline coating; water used in all final concrete; water supplied to or generated on platforms; water used for cooling; water used on supply vessels and tugs	Water used at minor construction sites where modules, single-point or single-buoy mooring systems are constructed; water required on tankers; water used to make the initial metal products; etc.
Energy	Energy used to operate all vessels, helicopters, and cranes directly involved in assembly and installation of facilities; energy used for seismic and exploration work; energy for transporting materials and pipes to construction sites and to offshore locations; energy to fabricate and install final facilities including modules and deck; energy used for pile driving	Energy used to transport personnel to construction sites on land; energy sequestered in prefinished materials
Land	Major construction sites for platforms, shore bases, pipe storage, vessel berths, and helicopter bases	Ocean floor used for platform and offshore terminal sites; module construction sites and sites where subassemblies are manufactured
Manpower	Personnel required to operate seismic and exploration rigs, supply vessels, tugs, cranes, barges, and helicopters; personnel to fabricate and install modules, decks, platforms, pipelines, and other facilities; labor required for transport of materials and pipes to construction sites or offshore locations	Labor to manufacture prefinished material such as ingots of steel, aluminum and copper, and subassemblies used in modules and elsewhere
Materials	All major material items required within the facilities themselves, and necessary consumable items required at the major sites to construct or install facilities, such as drill bits, chemicals, exploration well casings, blowout preventor, site buildings, and storage silos	Capital equipment material that will be employed for a limited duration, such as a lay barge, and small-quantity items as copper wire, silicon, etc.

[a] This table is by no means comprehensive, but it attempts to explain by examples the terms "direct" and "indirect" resource requirements. For specific details, see Chapter 6, Notes N000–707.

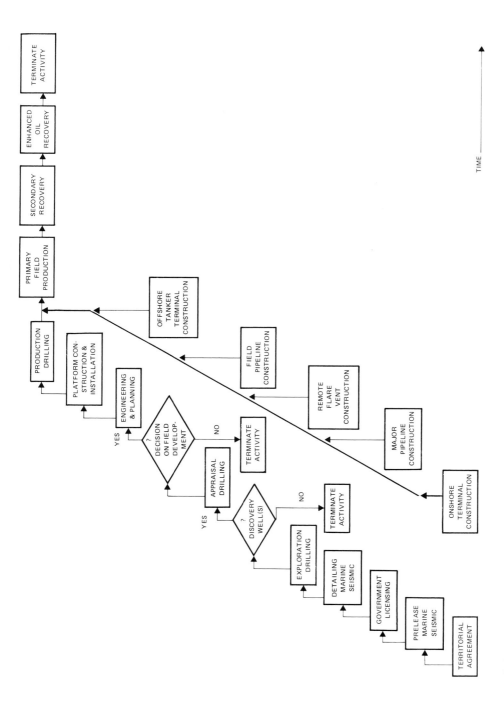

FIGURE 2.1   Simplistic diagram of activities generally necessary to develop a North Sea oil field.

9

TABLE 2.2 Commercial oil fields in production in the U.K. sector of the North Sea, as of July 1980.

Field	Operating company	Discovery date	Production start-up date	Estimated peak production rate ($\times 10^6$ tonnes/year)
Argyll	Hamilton Bros.	October 1971	June 1975	1.1
Auk	Shell	February 1971	February 1976	2.3
Beryl A	Mobil	September 1972	June 1976	5.0
Brent	Shell	July 1971	November 1976	23.0
Claymore	Occidental	May 1974	November 1977	4.5
Dunlin	Shell	July 1973	August 1978	5.9
Forties	BP	November 1970	November 1975	24.0
Heather	UNOCAL	December 1973	October 1978	1.7
Montrose	Amoco	September 1969	June 1976	1.4
Ninian	Chevron	January 1974	December 1978	17.7
Piper	Occidental	January 1973	December 1976	12.6
South Cormorant	Shell	September 1972	December 1979	3.0
Thistle	BNOC	July 1973	February 1978	8.7

[a] Including all production, subsea, and reinjection wells to be drilled from or near each platform, but excluding previously-drilled exploration and appraisal wells.
[b] Semi-submersible rig (Transworld 58) employed as a production platform.

TABLE 2.3 Commercial oil fields under development in the U.K. sector of the North Sea, as of July 1980.

Field	Operating company	Discovery date	Production start-up date	Estimated peak production rate ($\times 10^6$ tonnes/year)
Beatrice	BNOC	September 1976	1981	3.9
Brae	Marathon	April 1975	1983	4.9
Buchan	BP	August 1974	1980	2.2
Fulmar	Shell/Esso	November 1975	1981	8.6
Hutton	Conoco	September 1973	1984	5.7
Magnus	BP	March 1974	1983	5.9
Maureen	Philips	February 1973	1982	4.0
Murchison	Conoco	September 1975	1980	7.2[f]
North Cormorant	Shell/Esso	July 1974	1982	7.3
North West Hutton	Amoco	April 1975	1982	5.1
Tartan	Texaco	December 1974	1980	4.0

[a] Including all production, subsea, and reinjection wells to be drilled from or near each platform, but excluding previously-drilled exploration and appraisal wells.
[b] Two steel platforms plus one jack-up (Zapata Nordic).
[c] Semi-submersible rig (Drillmaster).

Estimated recoverable reserves ($\times 10^6$ tonnes)	Water depth (m)	Number of platforms (type)	Number of wells anticipated[a]
4.5	79	1[b]	11
8.0	84	1 (steel)	9
66.0	117	1 (concrete)	41
229.0[c,d]	140	4 (1 steel, 3 concrete)	136
55.0	110	1 (steel)	36
41.0[c]	151	1 (concrete)	45
240.0	104–128	4 (steel)	106
12.0–16.0	145	1 (steel)	40
12.1	90	1 (steel)	24
155.0	140	3 (2 steel, 1 concrete)	96
88.0	122	1 (steel)	26
12.0[c,e]	149	1 (concrete)	21
69.0	162	1 (steel)	61

[c] Total discounted reserves, that is, proven reserves plus suitable discounted figures for probable and possible reserves.
[d] Stabilized crude oil, excluding natural-gas liquids, for Block 211/29.
[e] Data refer to production from Block 211/26a.

Estimated recoverable reserves ($\times 10^6$ tonnes)	Water depth (m)	Number of platforms (type)	Number of wells anticipated[a]
21.0	45	3 (steel)[b]	37
36.0	103	1 (steel)	36
6.8	120	1 (steel)[c]	7
70.0	72	2 (steel)	28
24.0–34.0	147	1 (steel)[d]	32
60.0	187	1 (steel)	22
21.0	98	1 (steel)[e]	19
51.0[f]	156	1 (steel)	25[g]
55.0	160	1 (steel)	32
37.5	144	1 (steel)	30
27.0	142	1 (steel)	30

[d] Tension-leg platform.
[e] Steel gravity platform.
[f] Production and reserve figures for whole field, including part which lies in Norwegian block 33/9.
[g] Including 3 exploration/appraisal wells drilled previously and re-used, 2 for production and 1 for water injection.

Figure 2.1 provides a simplistic diagram of the activities generally necessary to develop a North Sea oil field, but represents only the outline of the more-complex decision tree actually employed in the development process. It can be seen that the process of field development is complex and certainly not an easy task.

Tables 2.2 and 2.3 provide brief descriptions of the commercial oil fields in the U.K. sector of the North Sea that were included in the analyses and are reported here. Table 2.2 lists those fields which were in production as of July 1980, and Table 2.3 describes the fields under development at the same date.

EXPLORATION AND APPRAISAL DRILLING

858 exploration and appraisal wells were drilled in the U.K. sector of the North Sea from 1964 through July 1980. Of this total, only 144 wells have been allocated to the 23 fields under study. Allocation of the exploration and appraisal wells to the 23 fields was made on a field-by-field basis, using data provided by the operating companies. Consequently, it is likely that a significant proportion of the resources required to drill all the North Sea exploration wells will remain unaccounted for in any subsequent calculations, except for the details provided here in Table 2.4.

TABLE 2.4 Cumulative total (to July 1980) of the estimated direct resource requirements for drilling exploration and appraisal wells in the U.K. sector of the North Sea.

Resource (units)	Total requirements for exploration and appraisal drilling in	
	Entire U.K. sector[a]	23 Fields in production or under development[b]
Water ($\times$ 10^5 m^3)	196.74	33.02
Energy		
Electricity ($\times$ 10^5 GJe)	94.38	15.84
Motor fuels ($\times$ 10^5 GJ)	1973.40	331.20
Land (km^2)	1.62 (temporary)	0.27 (temporary)
Manpower (man-years)	123,380	20,707
Materials (tonnes)		
Steel	479,708	80,510
Cement	348,691	58,522
Chemicals	871,728	146,304

[a] Based on the 858 offshore exploration and appraisal wells drilled from 1964 through July 1980 in the U.K. sector.
[b] Based on the 144 discovery and appraisal wells necessary to determine the commercial viability of the 23 fields studied.

PLATFORMS

OFFSHORE DRILLING AND PRODUCTION PLATFORMS

The major facility in the North Sea is the production platform. From such platforms the deviated (non-vertical) production wells are drilled to the desired reservoir depths. Wells that are 100 ft. (30.5 m) apart at the platform can be up to 5 miles (8 km) apart at a reservoir depth (measured along the bore hole) of approximately 1.5 miles (2.4 km).

The design, construction, and installation of a platform occurs over a period of two to four years, depending on the structural design, type of platform, weather conditions, safety regulations, and labor disputes. The North Sea platform is designed to withstand the type of storm which occurs only once in a hundred years, with wave heights up to 100 ft. (30.5 m); it is also built for resistance to damage caused by sea-water oxidation and impact. Two basic types of platforms are used in the North Sea: the steel-jacket platform, attached to the sea bed through piling, and the concrete-gravity platform, whose enormous bulk allows it to remain stationary on the sea bed. An additional feature of the concrete platform is that it can provide the required offshore crude storage; the stored crude and/or sea water provide the ballast needed to retain the concrete structure in place.

A deck, which can be of concrete or steel, is fitted over the support structure. The deck, in turn, supports such equipment as drilling rigs, production and process equipment, living quarters, pipeline pumps, secondary recovery equipment, helipads, and communication facilities. This equipment is placed in modularized packages which can be installed at the coast prior to float-out (in the case of concrete platforms), or can be lifted onto the steel platform decks when the platform is piled to the sea bed at its permanent location. The modularization aids in reducing construction and installation time. Once the construction "tie-in" is made, the platform is commissioned, and production-well drilling can begin. The production wells are drilled in incremental groups to allow for early production of crude oil and consequently an early return on investment. In addition, sea-bed drilling conductors are being employed in the smaller fields. The conductor is placed on the sea bed while the jacket is being constructed, and the wells are then drilled from a mobile drilling ship or a semi-submersible drilling rig. When the platform is complete, it is placed over the conductor, and the wells are finally "tied-in" via the installed platform. Once again, this technique is designed to reduce the amount of time needed to start production from the field, and this allows for an earlier return on investment.

Tables 2.5 and 2.6 list some of the more important characteristics of the platforms in the U.K. sector of the North Sea installed to date or scheduled for installation prior to 1984. Table 2.5 deals with the steel platforms and Table 2.6 provides similar information for the concrete platforms.

DESIGN CRITERIA OF STEEL AND CONCRETE PLATFORMS

Figures 2.2 and 2.3 are the final results of an attempt to understand the design criteria for steel platforms. As shown in Table 2.5, the total weight of the steel platforms was evaluated relative to water depth at the platform site, number of well conductors (well slots), peak production rates, and anticipated lifetime production. Of those items evaluated, only the water depth and the number of well conductors show a reasonably consistent relationship to the total loaded weight of steel platforms in air.

TABLE 2.5 Steel platforms in use or scheduled for installation by 1984 in the U.K. sector of the North Sea.

Platform	Weights (tonnes) of			
	Structural steel	Deck	Modules and equipment	Piles
Argyll[d]	4,500	_e	2,300	–
Auk	3,360	450	5,000	1,960
Beatrice				
Drilling	4,600	_f	3,538	4,500
Production	4,300	_f	4,973	4,500
Jack-up (Zapata Nordic)	8,200	_f	_e	–
Brae	16,000	_f	31,000	11,600
Brent A	14,000	1,800	9,580	7,200
Buchan Semi-submersible				
(Drillmaster)	18,083	_f	3,000	–
Claymore	9,286	1,000	12,286	3,135
Forties				
FA (Graythorp I)	15,436	_f	10,551	6,428
FB (Graythorp II)	18,253	_f	10,551	7,417
FC (Highlands One)	18,398	_f	10,551	7,417
FD (Highlands Two)	16,892	_f	10,551	7,417
Fulmar				
Fulmar Main Jacket (A)	12,500	4,900	22,500	5,000
Fulmar Wellhead (B)	1,570	250	–	1,000
Hutton[i]	38,468[g]	_f	16,530	–
Magnus	40,700[h]	_f	30,800	12,240
Maureen	40,000	_f	16,200	–
Montrose	6,500	1,600	4,486	2,300
Murchison	18,900	5,000	24,000	8,544
Ninian				
Northern	17,000	_f	9,000	6,000
Southern	20,000	_f	17,497	8,000
North Cormorant	21,300	1,800	44,467	6,100
North West Hutton	16,000	1,372	25,700	6,500
Piper	12,972	1,089	5,715	8,016
Tartan A	17,000	1,400	18,600	8,400
Thistle	31,650	_f	25,930	13,000

[a] Total possible number of production, subsea, and water- and gas-injection wells; in other words, the total number of well conductors or well slots plus the subsea wells.

[b] Values given are based on the maximum specified capability of each platform, and assume 365 days/year of peak production. Generally, these data were obtained direct from the operating companies.

[c] Based on operators' estimates published (June 1980) by the U.K. Department of Energy, and assuming that the platform will last for the production lifetime of the field.

[d] Semi-submersible rig employed as a production platform.

Water depth (m)	Total number of wells[a]	Peak production rate of crude oil[b] ($\times 10^6$ tonnes/year)	Expected lifetime production[c] ($\times 10^6$ tonnes)	Storage capacity (barrels)
79	8	1.1	4.5	—
84	12	2.3	8.0	—
45	32	—	—	—
45	—	3.1	16.0	—
45	12	0.8	5.0	—
103	46	4.9	36.0	—
140	28	4.86	41.0	—
120	11	2.2	6.8	12,000
110	36	4.5	55.0	—
106	27	6.2	60.0	—
122	26	6.2	60.0	—
127	27	6.2	60.0	—
122	26	6.2	60.0	—
82	36	8.6	70.0	—
82	6	—	—	—
147	32	5.7	24.0–34.0	—
187	27	5.9	60.0	—
98	19	4.0	21.0	650,000
90	24	1.4	12.0	—
156	30	7.2[i]	51.0[i]	—
140	24	3.93	34.4	—
140	42	6.88	60.3	—
160	40	7.3	55.0	—
144	40	5.1	37.5	—
122	36	12.6	88.0	—
142	33	4.0	27.0	—
162	70	8.7	69.0	70,000

[e] Included in the weight of structural steel.
[f] These decks are integral parts of the modules and/or the platforms.
[g] Including vessel, risers, mooring lines, and anchors.
[h] Self-floating structure.
[i] Including production and reserve data for the part of the Murchison field which lies in the Norwegian sector.
[j] Floating tension-leg platform.

TABLE 2.6 Concrete platforms in use in the U.K. sector of the North Sea.

Platform	Weights (tonnes) of						Water depth (m)	Total number of wells[b]	Peak production of crude oil ($\times 10^6$ t/yr)[c]	Expected lifetime production ($\times 10^6$ t)[d]	Storage capacity (barrels)
	Structural steel	Reinforcing steel	Prestressed steel	Concrete[a]	Deck	Modules and equipment					
Beryl A	630	9,000	3,000	192,000	6,962	20,000	117	44	5.00	66.0	900,000
Brent											
B	900	10,000	1,600	153,770	3,100	11,590	140	38	7.79	66.0	1,100,000
C	—	14,000	1,100	267,900	6,400	13,280	140	40	7.30	61.0	550,000
D	630	14,000	1,400	158,970	3,200	11,200	140	48	7.30	61.0	1,100,000
Dunlin A	1,450	9,500	3,000	211,050	3,800	11,300	151	48	5.90	41.0	800,000
Ninian Central	10,000	30,000	—	356,000	15,000	45,000	140	42	6.88	60.3	—
South Cormorant A	—	13,500	1,000	275,500	4,500	13,000	149	36	3.00	12.0	1,000,000

[a] Excluding any grouting materials required for platform installation.
[b] Total possible number of production, subsea, and water- and gas-injection wells; in other words, the total number of well conductors or well slots plus the subsea wells.
[c] In million tonnes/year; values given are based on the maximum specified capability of each platform, and assume 365 days/year of peak production. Generally, these data were obtained direct from the operating companies.
[d] In million tonnes; based on operators' estimates published (June 1980) by the U.K. Department of Energy, and assuming that the platform will last for the production lifetime of the field.

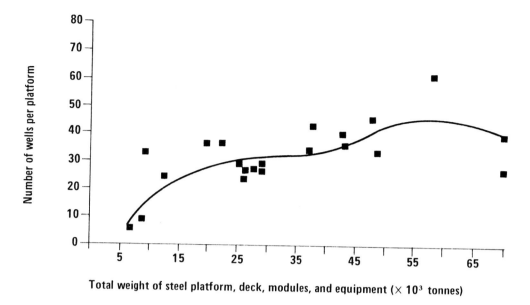

FIGURE 2.2 Relationship between total weight of steel platform and water depth.

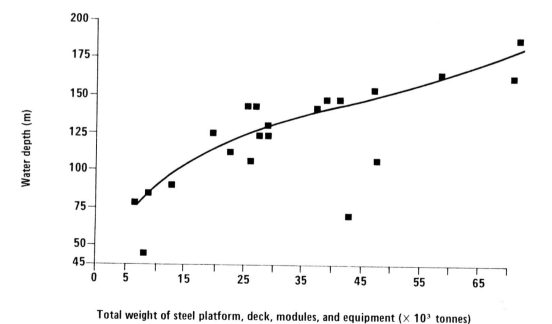

FIGURE 2.3 Relationship between total weight of steel platform and number of wells per platform.

A similar evaluation was conducted for the concrete production platforms installed or to be installed in U.K. waters. Table 2.6 summarizes the loaded weight in air of the concrete platforms, the water depth, the number of well conductors (well slots), anticipated lifetime production, and storage capacity. On comparing the various characteristics or potential design criteria to total loaded platform weight no reasonable correlation is found: some of the platforms that are quite heavy have low anticipated production rates, whereas some of the lightest concrete platforms have the highest storage capacities and are located in fairly deep water.

Several explanations may be advanced for the low degree of correlation: for example, South Cormorant A is designed to operate as a pumping platform as well as a production platform. However, the overall lack of correlation cannot be explained away other than by noting that (1) details of only seven platforms were available for evaluation; (2) the design specification of concrete platforms is limited and allows for a wide margin of custom design; (3) one or more of the platforms are designed to incorporate additional safety factors; and (4) the comparison includes two unique types of design, the general "condeep" design and the "outer and inner wall" concept used for the Ninian Central platform.

CONCRETE VERSUS STEEL PLATFORMS

One of the major items of discussion during the development of the North Sea fields has been the relative advantages of concrete and steel platforms. Table 2.7 and Figure 2.4 give details of a comparison of the direct resources necessary to construct a typical concrete and a typical steel platform in the North Sea*. When one compares the direct plus indirect energy requirements** for the construction of concrete versus steel platforms (72.415×10^5 GJ and 59.50×10^5 GJ, respectively) one finds that the concrete platform is more demanding to construct in terms of direct and indirect energy requirements. However, were one to include the capital energy needed to construct and install the platform (not evaluated in this study), one would probably find the two types of platform to be more nearly equal in terms of total energy consumed for construction and installation.

From the comparison, one finds that the concrete platform requires nearly the same quantity of steel as the steel platform itself, but of course a lower-quality steel. The land and water requirements for construction are nearly equal, although there does appear to be an advantage for the concrete platform in terms of labor requirements. However, a number of the operating companies which have installed concrete platforms and have seen the comparison think the number of man-years given in Table 2.7 for the construction of a concrete platform is slightly underestimated. Consequently, given all of the above, one can state that there appears to be no significant difference in the water, energy, land, and manpower resources required to construct a concrete or a steel platform, although the material requirements for the concrete platform are much higher. The major factor ignored in this statement is that the concrete platform can provide field storage capacity; thus, the concrete platform is quite a viable alternative for developing fields where major storage is required because of lack of access to a pipeline via a tie-in.

---

*The data required to define "typical" concrete and "typical" steel platforms are developed in Chapter 6. The characteristics of each type of platform were arrived at by averaging the data for 7 concrete and 13 steel platforms, installed to date and producing oil in the U.K. sector.

**Converting GJe values to GJ, assuming a generating efficiency of 33%.

18

DIRECT RESOURCES REQUIRED TO CONSTRUCT ONE STEEL AND ONE CONCRETE PLATFORM

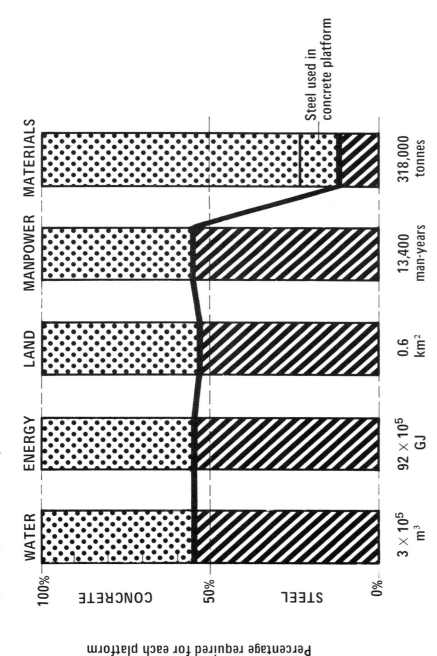

FIGURE 2.4 Comparison of the direct resources required to construct a "typical" concrete and a "typical" steel platform. (Note that energy values in GJe have been converted to GJ, assuming a generating efficiency of 33%, before inclusion in the figure.)

TABLE 2.7 Concrete versus steel: a comparison of the direct resources required to construct a typical concrete and a typical steel platform in the North Sea[a].

Resource (units)	Total direct requirements for a	
	Concrete platform	Steel platform
Water ($\times 10^5$ m^3)	1.249	1.437
Energy		
Electricity ($\times 10^5$ GJe)	15.937	11.340
Motor fuels ($\times 10^5$ GJ)	2.641	6.090
Process-heat fuels ($\times 10^5$ GJ)	0.273	0.820
Land (km^2)	0.276	0.325
Manpower (man-years)	5,928	7,424
Materials (tonnes)		
Structural steel	22,719	37,027
Reinforcing steel	11,000	–
Prestressed steel	1,500	–
Concrete	240,506	4,777

[a] Installed in water depths of 104–162 m.

PRODUCTION WELLS

The directionally-drilled oil-production wells sunk from the North Sea platforms generally range from 10,100 to 14,750 ft. (3078–4496 m) in depth, measured along the bore hole. An average of 73 days is required to drill one such well. The casing string for an 11,000-ft. (3353 m) well is composed of some 720 tonnes of steel, while the blowout preventor, drill bits, drill pipe, and other drilling equipment account for another 165 tonnes of steel per well. In addition, nearly 940 tonnes of cement and chemicals are needed for the successful completion of the 11,000-ft. well [3].

Production-well drilling has dominated North Sea development activity over the period 1977–1980. The total number of North Sea wells completed annually rose from 72 in 1976 to 107 in 1979. Over the last three years, production-well drilling has accounted for an average of approximately 70% of the total amount of drilling in the U.K. sector.

The total cumulative number of production, injection, and subsea wells expected to be drilled for the 23 fields studied here is 907; to date, approximately 629 offshore oil-development wells have been drilled throughout the entire U.K. sector. Clifton A. Brown of the Riggs National Bank has estimated [22] that a total of 1722 production wells will have been drilled in all sectors of the North Sea over the period 1976–1989.

PIPELINES

TRANSPORT OF HYDROCARBONS RECOVERED OFFSHORE

There are two alternative methods for transporting oil from the fields to the coast: either the oil can be loaded into tankers at sea, via several types of offshore loading terminals, or it can be piped to shore. In the case of gas in large quantities, pipelines are the only practical method. A large number of combinations are employed in the transport of oil in the North Sea. In the initial stages of field development, tankers may be loaded either directly from the wellhead, from the storage facilities at the platform, or from offshore-terminal loading facilities. Once a particular offshore pipeline is constructed to serve several fields that are in various stages of development, the offshore terminal is removed and the crude is shipped via the pipeline. In those cases where the quantity of oil to be recovered is small and the field is remote, it is uneconomical to lay an offshore pipeline. For such fields the transport of crude will be via an offshore terminal with some storage capacity to match production to the rate of removal by tanker.

The amount of offshore storage found in the fields developed to date varies widely. For those fields (such as Argyll) where buoy mooring systems are used for direct tanker loading, no offshore storage exists. In contrast, for those fields that employ the massive concrete platforms, there is up to 1.1 million barrels of storage (Brent B and Brent D) internal to the platform itself.

There are two systems of offshore pipelines, intra-field pipelines and inter-field pipelines. Intra-field pipelines transmit crude and/or gas to offshore loading terminals, to other production platforms, or from subsea wells to production platforms (see Table 2.8). Such

TABLE 2.8 Major North Sea crude oil pipelines[a].

Pipeline	Length (miles)	Outside diameter (in.)	Operator	Year commissioned	Remarks
Ekofisk–Teesside	220.0	34	Phillips	1975	Originates in Norwegian waters
Forties–Cruden Bay	110.0	32	BP	1975	
Piper–Flotta	124.0	30	Occidental	1976	
South Cormorant–Sullom Voe	93.0	36	Shell/Esso	1978	Will serve Brent and other fields
Ninian–Sullom Voe	105.0	36	BP	1978	
Claymore–Piper Trunkline	8.0	30	Occidental	1977	
Dunlin–South Cormorant	17.0	24	Shell	1978	
Thistle–Dunlin	7.0	16	BODL Ltd.	1978	
Heather–Ninian	22.0	16	Union Oil	1978	
Brent–South Cormorant	22.0	30	Shell	1979	
Beatrice–Old Sandwick	45.0	16	BNOC	–	
Murchison–Dunlin	10.0	16	Conoco	–	
Hutton–North West Hutton	4.0	12.75	Conoco	–	
North West Hutton–South Cormorant A	7.5	20	Amoco	–	
Brae–Forties	70.2	24	Marathon	–	
North Cormorant–South Cormorant A	10.6	20	Shell	–	
Magnus–Ninian	57.0	24	BP	–	
Tartan–Claymore	16.8	24	Texaco	–	

[a] Data from the U.K. Department of Energy publication, *Development of the Oil and Gas Resources of the United Kingdom* (1980), and private communications with the operating companies.

pipelines range in size from 4.5 to 24 in. outside diameter. The inter-field pipelines, which are generally larger (16—36 in. outside diameter), transport the crude from one field to another, or from the field to the terminal facilities onshore.

The laying of an offshore pipeline is a demanding task. The steel pipe is first coated onshore with a protective coating of concrete made from a mixture of cement, iron ore, heavy aggregates, and steel reinforcement. The iron ore and heavy aggregates give the desired additional weight to hold the submerged pipeline in place. The transported pipes, in sections 12 and/or 24 m in length, are welded together on a lay barge and the "string" is lowered into the sea. The lay barge moves forward slowly by winching and paying out its anchors. After the pipe string has been laid on the sea floor, it is trenched into the sea bed for protection against subsea currents and anchors. Submarine inspections and pressure tests follow the burying operation.

As of July 1980, a total of 2192 miles (3528 km) of oil and gas pipelines in the U.K. sector were commissioned, awaiting commissioning, or under construction. This total is composed of 950 miles (1529 km) of major offshore crude oil lines, 70 miles (113 km) of intra-field crude oil lines, and 1172 miles (1886 km) of major gas lines.

Table 2.9 depicts, in summary form, the resource requirements for constructing the major crude oil pipelines of the North Sea and the field pipelines of the U.K. sector. The field pipelines are those that connect the various field production platforms to remote flare vents, to subsea wells, to offshore-terminal loading facilities, and to other production platforms, etc.

TABLE 2.9 Estimated direct resource requirements for constructing the crude oil pipelines of the U.K. sector[a].

Resource (units)	Direct requirements for		
	Major export pipelines	Intra-field pipelines	All export and intra-field pipelines[a]
Water (m³)	347,846	26,287	374,133
Energy			
Electrical ($\times 10^5$ GJe)	31.047	2.439	33.486
Motor fuels ($\times 10^5$ GJ)	185.595	14.524	200.119
Process-heat fuels ($\times 10^5$ GJ)	1.776	0.139	1.915
Land[b] (km²)	1.023	0.097	1.12
Manpower (man-years)	16,069	1,272	17,341
Materials (tonnes)			
Rolled steel	355,057	25,146	380,203
Reinforcing steel	35,643	2,594	38,237
Cement	110,276	8,126	118,402
Iron ore	187,035	13,184	200,219
Sand	179,886	13,255	193,141
Asphalt	93,657	7,317	100,974

[a] Data in the table exclude the requirements for the Ekofisk—Teesside pipeline which, although it passes through the U.K. sector, carries crude oil from the Norwegian sector.

[b] Including temporary land requirements on shore for equipment, material, and office placement, but excluding areas used on the sea bed.

TOTAL RESOURCE REQUIREMENTS FOR FIELD DEVELOPMENT

SUMMARY OF RESOURCE REQUIREMENTS

In the preceding sections of this chapter, we have discussed the resource requirements necessary for the major phases of field development, e.g., exploration and appraisal drilling, and platform and pipeline construction. The tables and figures which follow summarize the total resources necessary to develop the 23 fields of the U.K. sector. It is emphasized that a field is considered to be under development until all production wells have been drilled and the production rate has reached its maximum. For some of the fields evaluated, this situation will not occur until 1981–1985.

Also, it should be stressed that, in general, only the direct resource requirements are given in the following tables*. Consequently, there are additional indirect and capital requirements which are not reported here. Only in the case of energy requirements was a complete analysis conducted (see Tables 2.11–2.13).

Table 2.10 gives the total direct construction requirements to develop the 23 commercial oil fields in the U.K. sector of the North Sea, and Figure 2.5 provides a graphical description of the total weight of materials necessary to develop the fields. In Figure 2.5, the sizes of the rectangles (drawn to scale) represent the total amount of direct material necessary for development; final electricity demand was converted to tonnes of coal equivalent to allow for its direct inclusion in the figure. It should be noted that there is an additional requirement of 28.7 million tonnes of fresh and salt water necessary for development as intake water, but this is not shown in Figure 2.5. Also, a cumulative total of 333,000 man-years of direct labor will have been required to develop the fields by 1984–1985.

ENERGY ANALYSIS OF FIELD DEVELOPMENT AND OPERATION

Table 2.10 and Figure 2.5 provided some insight into the total direct energy required for field development. It also seemed useful to evaluate the direct, indirect, and capital components of the total energy requirement, and the results of this evaluation are given in Tables 2.11–2.13. Table 2.11 illustrates how the indirect sequestered energy was derived for the analysis. The data in Table 2.12 were calculated from the direct energies shown in Table 2.10, and the indirect energies of Table 2.11. Hence, from Table 2.12 one can gain an understanding of the total energy required to produce one tonne of North Sea oil from a fully-operational well, and to transfer it to shore via a pipeline.

When all exploration, appraisal, construction, and production requirements are included, this study arrives at a total energy requirement for recovering North Sea oil and transporting it to shore of 0.8122 GJ/tonne**, which is only 1.85% of the calorific value of the oil recovered. It should be emphasized that this represents only the *energy* requirements necessary to develop the field; manpower, material, water, and land requirements are additional

---

*For a clarification of the terms "direct" and "indirect" resources, and details of how the data were aggregated to form some of the subsequent tables, the reader is referred to the introduction to this chapter, where the terms and methods of compilation are described.

**The value 0.8122 GJ/tonne is composed of 0.3415 GJ/tonne direct energy, 0.1084 GJ/tonne indirect energy, 0.0724 GJ/tonne capital energy, 0.1637 GJ/tonne operating energy to produce the oil, and 0.1262 GJ/tonne to transport it to shore. The recoverable reserves assumed in the calculation are 1393.9×10^6 tonnes of oil; this excludes the reserves of Heather field.

TABLE 2.10 Total anticipated direct construction requirements[a] for developing the oil fields in the U.K. sector which are deemed commercially viable as of July 1980.

Resource (units)	Direct construction requirements						
	Seismic survey	Exploration	Platforms	Pipelines	Production wells	Offshore terminals	Flare vents
Water ($\times 10^5$ m³)	0.588	33.02	48.973	3.741	199.600	0.180	1.146
Energy							
Electricity ($\times 10^5$ GJe)	–	15.84	429.079	33.496	143.600	1.17	1.565
Motor fuels ($\times 10^5$ GJ)	37.143	331.20	189.007	200.119	2092.200	0.416	1.584
Process-heat fuels ($\times 10^5$ GJ)	–	–	24.311	1.915	8.559	–	0.009
Land (km²)	0.87[b]	0.27[b]	11.03[b]	1.12[b]	1.902[b]	negligible	negligible
Manpower (man-years)	3,046	20,707	249,368	17,341	41,083	920	270
Materials (tonnes)							
Structural steel	negligible	80,510	1,192,428[c]	–	840,589	78,941	4,760
Reinforcing steel	–	–	100,000[c]	38,237	–	–	–
Prestressed steel	–	–	11,100[c]	–	–	–	–
Concrete	–	–	1,615,190[c]	–	–	624[d]	15,000
Cement[e]	–	58,522	–	118,402	386,486	–	–
Chemicals	–	146,304	–	–	504,981	–	–
Pipeline steel	–	–	–	380,203	–	–	–
Iron ore	–	–	–	200,219	–	–	–
Sand[f]	–	–	–	193,141	–	–	–
Asphalt	–	–	–	100,974	–	–	–
Ballast[g]	–	–	52,980[c]	–	–	18,600	–

[a] Excluding resource requirements for existing or newly-constructed tankers, onshore terminals, pipelines, or refineries.
[b] All onshore land use is assumed to be temporary.
[c] Materials needed to construct and install the platforms; the weights of the substructure, deck, modules, equipment, and piles are included as applicable. 95% of the modules and equipment are assumed to be made of high-carbon steel alloys. These data were obtained direct from the operating companies, and do not rely on the material requirements for "typical" concrete and "typical" steel platforms as developed in Table 2.7 and Chapter 6.
[d] Excluding the weight of concrete for the Maureen field terminal loading system, for which data are not yet available.
[e] Note that cement indicated is only that used to set the casing string and for pipeline coating. All the other cement is accounted for and included in the values for concrete.
[f] Excluding sand required to build graving docks to construct the platforms.
[g] Ballast used includes barytes, iron ore, and/or concrete.

TABLE 2.11 Energy sequestered within the materials utilized for the development of the oil fields in the U.K. sector.

Material	Weight (tonnes)	Gross energy requirement per tonne (GJ)[a]	Total gross energy requirement ($\times 10^5$ GJ)[a]
Structural steel	2,197,000	50.0	1098.5
Reinforcing steel	138,000	50.0	69.0
Prestressed steel	11,000	50.0	5.5
Pipeline steel	380,000	50.0	190.0
Concrete	1,631,000	1.7	27.7
Cement	563,000	8.0	45.0
Chemicals	651,000	8.0	52.1
Iron ore	200,000	1.3	2.6
Sand	193,000	0.5	1.0
Asphalt coating	101,000	18.9	19.1
Ballast	71,000	1.3	0.9
Total	6,136,000		1511.4

[a] The gross energy requirement is the sum of all the energy sources that must be sequestered to make a product available.

TABLE 2.12 Estimate of the total energy requirements for developing and operating the oil fields in the U.K. sector which are deemed commercially viable as of July 1980.

Energy requirement	Total construction energy requirements ($\times 10^5$ GJ)[a]			Operational energy requirements (GJ/tonne)[b]
	Direct	Indirect	Capital	
Electricity	1874.250×10^5 GJ[a]	_[c]	_[c]	—
Motor fuels	2851.669×10^5 GJ	_[c]	_[c]	0.2899
Process-heat fuels	34.794×10^5 GJ	_[c]	_[c]	—
Materials	—	1511.4[d]	—	—
Capital	—	—	1009.567[e]	—
Total	4760.713×10^5 GJ[a]	1511.4	1009.567	0.2899

[a] Assuming an electrical requirement of 624.750×10^5 GJe, generated at a fuel-to-electricity conversion efficiency of 33%.

[b] The operational requirements are composed of the energy required to produce the oil (0.1637 GJ/tonne) and to transport it to shore via a pipeline (0.1262 GJ/tonne).

[c] Unable to estimate the indirect and capital requirements.

[d] Gross energy requirement for materials (see Table 2.11).

[e] Capital energy requirements are based, in part, on the work of Hemming [26] and Macleod [27], that is, the percentage of capital energy cost versus direct energy costs.

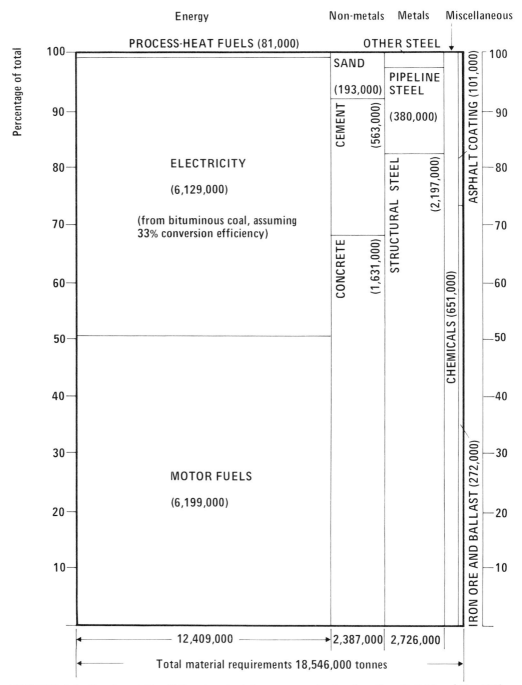

FIGURE 2.5 Total weight of direct materials necessary to develop the oil fields of the U.K. sector of the North Sea.

TABLE 2.13 Comparison of published estimates of the energy required to produce North Sea crude oil and transport it to shore.

Source	Energy required for production and transport (GJ/tonne)[a]	Recoverable reserves of crude oil assumed by each author ($\times 10^6$ tonnes)
Hemming [26] (Auk field only)	0.5580	13.3
Hemming [26] (Forties field only)	0.4572	245.0–272.0
Macleod [27] (Forties field only)	0.6022	272.0
This work (U.K. sector, including Murchison but excluding Statfjord)	0.8122	1393.9

[a] Including all direct, indirect, and capital energy costs of producing the oil, transporting it onshore, and transferring it to a refining facility.

resource expenses to be incurred. Further, the energy construction costs of the Sullom Voe and Flotta terminals have not been included, and each of the resource categories has its own indirect component, as does energy. However, it is clear that the expenditure of energy resources for the development of the crude oil fields of the North Sea is a wise investment, and the return is rapid. As illustrated earlier in Figure 2.5, the total direct energy requirement is equal to 6.1 million tonnes of coal equivalent plus 6.2 million tonnes of motor fuels; this corresponds to a pay-back period of 33 days at peak oil production rates (115×10^6 tonnes/year).

Finally, the results of the total energy analysis were compared to the published values developed by Hemming [26] and Macleod [27], as shown in Table 2.13.

factor relates the often cautiously-announced reserves and expected production rates with the actual quantities of oil produced over a number of years: the lower the appreciation factor, the more accurate was the original estimate. Some believe that the improved marine-seismic techniques employed in the North Sea will result in a low appreciation factor, but this too is a point of much debate.

The ultimate recovery rate (the percentage finally recovered out of the total resources originally found in place) may be higher than originally anticipated as new, improved techniques in enhanced oil recovery (see Chapter 4) are applied. As the value of crude oil continues to rise, the use of more-costly technology becomes a viable proposition.

In conclusion, there is still much speculation as to the size of the ultimate recoverable reserves in the North Sea, but one can state that the North Sea oil deposits are very significant relative to the national demands of the United Kingdom and Norway. In addition, there is the possibility that the ultimate reserves may be greater than some of the more moderate current estimates.

4 POTENTIAL FOR SECONDARY AND ENHANCED OIL RECOVERY IN THE NORTH SEA

In this chapter an attempt is made to understand the potential for secondary and enhanced (or "tertiary") oil recovery in the North Sea basin. An energy analysis was carried out to estimate the increased energy requirements to obtain one tonne of North Sea oil using secondary and enhanced oil-recovery techniques as compared to the primary recovery methods presently employed in the North Sea. The summarized results presented here are taken from a cooperative study by the author and Dr. Robert J. Peckham of the Joint Research Center, Commission of the European Communities, Ispra, Italy.

PRIMARY OIL RECOVERY

Primary oil recovery is the reliance upon natural energy forms in the reservoir for the production of crude oil. Such natural energy forms include natural water drive, the expansion of free gas, oil, water, and solution gas, and capillary and gravitational forces.

To make possible the primary recovery of oil from the North Sea basin, a large amount of resources have been and are being expended in exploration, platform and pipeline construction, production-well drilling, and the production process itself, as described in Chapter 2. Because of this large resource expenditure for primary recovery, it seems important to extend the evaluation to examine whether larger quantities of oil can be obtained for the resources already expended or to be expended.

SECONDARY OIL RECOVERY

Secondary oil recovery involves the introduction of energy into a reservoir by injecting gas or water under pressure. Separate wells are usually used for injection and production. The added energy stimulates the movement of the oil, providing additional recovered amounts at increased recovery rates.

In the North Sea, the injection of sea water will be the main secondary recovery method. As shown in Table 4.1, water injection is being used or is planned in almost all of the North Sea fields currently producing oil. The reinjection of natural gas is being used primarily as a means of storing the gas for later use and generally not as an aid to oil production. Consequently, in the energy analysis described later in this chapter, the energy needed

TABLE 4.1 Secondary recovery plans for 13 oil-producing fields in the U.K. sector of the North Sea.

Field	Water injection planned?	Estimated recoverable reserves ($\times 10^6$ tonnes)
Argyll[a]	No	4.5
Auk[a]	Questionable	8
Beryl A	Yes	66
Brent	Yes	229
Claymore	Yes	55
Dunlin	Yes	41
Forties	Yes	240
Heather	Yes	14
Montrose	Yes	12
Ninian	Yes	155
Piper	Yes	88
South Cormorant	Yes	12
Thistle	Yes	69

[a] During 1980, Argyll and Auk fields continued to experience "watering out" problems, that is, water levels are advancing in their oil-producing reservoirs. This factor, combined with the relatively low recoverable reserves, makes water-injection programs unlikely for both fields.

for gas reinjection will not be counted as a requirement for obtaining oil by secondary production methods.

ENHANCED OIL RECOVERY (TERTIARY PRODUCTION METHODS)*

Enhanced oil recovery or tertiary production encompasses thermal methods, carbon-dioxide flooding, and chemical flooding (using surfactants to reduce surface tension and ease the passage of oil through the rock, and using polymers to improve the efficiency of water injection). All these methods are still in the experimental stage for land-based fields and it is not known whether they will be used in the North Sea. However, it is possible to make some general observations regarding tertiary recovery in the North Sea and then to make a tentative estimate of the possible energy requirements. Thermal methods are unlikely to be used in the North Sea for two reasons. Firstly, they are best suited to higher-viscosity crudes and the crude found in the North Sea is of low viscosity. Secondly, thermal methods are considered unsuitable for field depths greater than ~3000 ft. (914 m), because of the associated cooling problems. Thus it seems that carbon-dioxide or chemical flooding are the only candidates for tertiary recovery in the North Sea. We consider chemical flooding to be the more likely choice, as it is known to be suitable for use after a water-injection program, and, as stated above, water injection is being used in most of the North Sea fields currently in production.

_____

*The terms "enhanced" and "tertiary" will be used interchangeably throughout this chapter.

ANALYSIS OF ENERGY REQUIREMENTS FOR SECONDARY AND TERTIARY PRODUCTION

The analysis was carried out using the data, presented in Chapter 2, on the total resources (including energy) necessary to develop the 13 oil-producing fields (excluding Statfjord) and the 11 fields under development in the U.K. sector. As discussed in Chapter 2, these data showed that the average gross energy requirement for crude-oil production using primary recovery methods is 0.8122 GJ/tonne; this value includes all the direct, indirect, and capital energy costs of producing the oil, transporting it to the shore, and transferring it to a refining facility. From this starting point, our next steps were to understand and then estimate the additional energy requirements for secondary and then for enhanced or tertiary oil-recovery techniques.

SECONDARY PRODUCTION

In order to calculate the increasing energy requirement as secondary production is phased in, it is necessary to know what quantities of oil can ultimately be attributed to secondary production (over and above that amount which would have been obtained by primary production alone), and then to allocate the additional energy inputs accordingly. We will begin by defining the more important parameters:

Let T = total oil in place ($\times 10^6$ tonnes)
R = recoverable reserves ($\times 10^6$ tonnes)
r_p = fraction of T recoverable using primary methods alone
$r_{p,s}$ = fraction of T recoverable using both primary and secondary methods
r_s = additional fraction of T recoverable using secondary methods ($= r_{p,s} - r_p$)
E_i = initial energy requirement in the field for construction of platforms, pipelines, etc. (GJ)
E_p^{prod} = ongoing energy requirement for primary production (GJ/tonne)
E^{trans} = energy requirement for transporting crude from field to shore (GJ/tonne)

The value for the recoverable reserves, R, is normally quoted assuming that both primary and secondary recovery will take place. Therefore,

$$R = r_{p,s}T \tag{1}$$

Since the initial energy requirement E_i covers equipment and facilities which are used in both the primary and secondary phases, an amount of energy $(10^{-6}/R)E_i$ must be included in the total energy requirement per tonne of oil produced in each phase; the factor 10^{-6} is introduced to relate the recoverable reserves (in units of 10^6 tonnes) to the energy requirements (in GJ/tonne). Thus, the total energy required (GJ/tonne) for primary production, E_p^{tot}, is given by

$$E_p^{tot} = (10^{-6}/R)E_i + E_p^{prod} + E^{trans} \tag{2}$$

To extend the argument to cover secondary production, we define three additional parameters:

E_s = additional energy requirement for constructing secondary production facilities (GJ)

E_s^{prod} = additional ongoing energy requirement for secondary production (GJ/tonne); because E_s^{prod} can vary with time, we will write it as $E_s^{prod}(t)$

A = total amount of oil recovered during secondary production phase (tonnes)

During secondary production, we assume that a certain fraction, r_{inj}, of the total oil recovered can be attributed to water injection, whereas the remaining fraction, $1 - r_{inj}$, is produced by natural forces. Also, by definition, and introducing the factor 10^6 so that we can equate the units of A and T,

$$r_{inj}A = r_s T 10^6$$

which may be rearranged as

$$r_{inj} = 10^6 r_s T/A \tag{3}$$

The energy required to extract each tonne of the fraction attributable to water injection has three components: the total energy requirement for primary production E_p^{tot}, a proportion of the energy needed to construct secondary production facilities, and the additional ongoing energy requirement for secondary production E_s^{prod}. To derive the second of these components, we divide the total construction requirement E_s by the amount of recovered oil attributable to water injection alone, which is $r_{inj}A$ or [from eqn. (3)] $10^6 r_s T$. Summing these components gives us a requirement (in GJ/tonne) of $E_p^{tot} + (10^{-6}E_s/r_sT) + E_s^{prod}(t)$ for the fraction attributable to water injection. Since the remaining fraction, $1 - r_{inj}$, requires E_p^{tot} (GJ/tonne) to extract, we can now write an equation for the total energy E_s^{tot} (GJ/tonne) required for secondary production:

$$E_s^{tot} = (1 - r_{inj})E_p^{tot} + r_{inj}\left[E_p^{tot} + \left(\frac{10^{-6}E_s}{r_sT}\right) + E_s^{prod}(t)\right]$$

which simplifies to give

$$E_s^{tot} = E_p^{tot} + r_{inj}\left[\frac{10^{-6}E_s}{r_sT} + E_s^{prod}(t)\right] \tag{4}$$

For all the fields studied, estimates of the recoverable reserves, R, were obtained from the operating companies. In some cases estimates were also available for T, the total oil in place; where this value was not available it was calculated from eqn. (1), using either the quoted value of $r_{p,s}$ or an assumed value of $r_{p,s} = 0.41$ (the average of all available estimates of $r_{p,s}$). In very few cases was a value for r_p available, so in general an assumed value of $r_p = 0.2$ was used.

A production profile was constructed for each field using the operators' estimates of the date when production started or will start, and the time, duration, and magnitude of peak production. An exponential decay rate of 10% per annum was used for the declining phase.

The most important contribution to the additional energy investment in secondary production, E_s, is the provision of extra wells for the injection of water. Using the data collected for this book, an energy analysis for a typical well [11,000 ft. (3353 m) measured along the bore hole] was made and this was used in conjunction with available drilling data to calculate E_s for each field. Accurate values for the planned numbers of production and water-injection wells were available, as well as details of the numbers of wells to be drilled in a given year.

Further assumptions had to be made in order to estimate $E_s^{prod}(t)$. For most fields there is some uncertainty regarding the timing of the onset of water injection, the volume of water to be pumped, and the pumping pressure. These parameters depend on characteristics of the field which can only be ascertained once production is under way. For example, the Piper field has been found to have a substantial natural aquifer, and may not now need additional water injection, while in the Forties field water injection is already taking place. However, it is possible to make some general deductions from the available information. For example, in all cases where water-injection equipment is installed on a platform, the capacity of the equipment, in barrels of water per day, is equal to or slightly greater than the estimated peak production of the field, in barrels of oil per day. In the case of the Auk field it is estimated that water injection of 70,000 barrels per day may be needed throughout the life of the field, while peak production of oil is estimated at only 50,000 barrels per day. Therefore it is reasonable to assume that, on average, the rate of water injection continues at a maximum value, while oil production declines in the later stages. Knowing the flow rate, the pressure, and the pump efficiency, the energy requirement for pumping can be calculated. The manufacturers' quoted pump efficiencies ranged from 28 to 32%; a figure of 30% was used in our analysis. An injection pressure of 1250 p.s.i. (8.6×10^6 Pa) at the surface was assumed throughout.

For each of the oil-producing fields studied, a profile for the energy requirement was constructed using eqns. (2) and (4) for the primary and secondary production phases, respectively. The weighted average energy requirement was then calculated for each field. This study showed that, on average, an additional 0.154 GJ/tonne will be required to produce oil via secondary techniques.

TERTIARY PRODUCTION

As already stated, it is not yet known whether tertiary production will be used in the North Sea or what its results would be. Consequently the analysis for this stage is very simple and is based on available data for chemical-injection programs in other parts of the world. Most information is available for fields in the U.S.A., where chemical injection is being used to follow secondary water injection. The different estimates given in the literature [3,4] for the possible increase in recovery factor when tertiary methods are used range from 5 to 20%. For the 13 oil-producing fields under consideration, these estimates would correspond to an extra cumulative production of 50×10^6 to 200×10^6 tonnes.

The best available estimates* for the requirements in chemicals per additional barrel of oil produced are 4.54 ± 0.76 kg petroleum sulfonates, 1.36 kg alcohols, and 0.45 ± 0.11 kg

---

*Chemicals for Microemulsion Flooding in Enhanced Oil Recovery, Report No. 159, Gulf Universities Research Consortium, Bellair, Texas, February 1977.

polymers. In energy terms these chemical inputs correspond to an extra 1.78–3.19 GJ per additional tonne of oil produced. If we assume the ongoing energy requirements for platform operation, pumping, etc., are the same as in the secondary phase, then this range of uncertainty in the energy requirement for chemicals is 2 orders of magnitude greater than other conceivable energy inputs (such as the energy required to transport the chemicals by sea from the U.K. to the platform).

To summarize our estimates of the possibilities for enhanced oil recovery in the North Sea, we can state that the additional cumulative production from the 13 oil-producing fields studied will range from a minimum of 50×10^6 to a maximum of 200×10^6 tonnes of oil. Similarly, the additional gross energy requirement, over and above that needed for secondary production, will range from a minimum of 2.75 to a maximum of 4.16 GJ per tonne of oil extracted.

CONCLUSIONS

When using primary methods, the average gross energy requirement to produce one tonne of oil from the U.K. offshore oil fields, transport it to the shore, and transfer it to a refinery is 0.8122 GJ. To produce a similar tonne of oil using secondary methods requires 0.9662 GJ, or 1.2 times the energy cost of primary production. Using enhanced oil-production techniques and the existing oil-production facilities requires a total average gross energy of between 2.75 and 4.16 GJ/tonne; this represents 3.4–5.1 times the energy cost of primary production.

However, it must be borne in mind that the maximum energy requirement to recover oil via enhanced techniques still represents only 10% of the calorific value of the crude oil produced. For this expenditure of energy, between 50×10^6 and 200×10^6 tonnes of crude oil could be recovered. Consequently, from our initial evaluation it would appear that the application of enhanced oil-recovery techniques to offshore production in the North Sea seems viable and certainly worthy of more detailed consideration.

5 NORTH SEA GAS VERSUS OIL: RESOURCE REQUIREMENTS FOR DEVELOPMENT

Natural gas was the first hydrocarbon to be discovered in the North Sea basin, when a large gas field was found near Groningen, the Netherlands, in 1959. The quest for oil and additional quantities of gas continued in earnest throughout the next two decades. There has always appeared to be more interest in searching for oil in the area rather than natural gas, although oil was not found in significant quantities until the discovery of the Ekofisk and Montrose fields in the late sixties. The greater interest in oil rather than gas can be explained, in part, by the fact that oil is a more flexible commodity. In comparison to natural gas, crude oil is subject to fewer governmental regulations, can be sold and transported beyond national borders with ease, has a standard world market price, and can be used as the starting point for a variety of finished products. However, natural gas has considerable potential to satisfy the increasing demand for energy as supplies of oil become depleted and alternative energy sources continue to be in the development stage. Consequently, it is desirable to understand the energy return on investment of resources required to develop and produce offshore natural gas, and to compare the requirements and returns with those of crude oil.

The Leman gas field has been selected as the basis for a comparison between North Sea gas and oil, and the two operators of the Leman field, Shell U.K. Ltd. [5] and Amoco U.K. [6], have kindly provided the necessary data.

HISTORY OF LEMAN GAS FIELD

The Leman gas field was discovered in April 1966, with an expected ultimate recovery of 10.52×10^{12} standard cubic ft. of natural gas. Approximately 47.3% of this total had been recovered by the beginning of 1980. The Leman field is the largest known gas deposit in the North Sea basin and one of the larger offshore gas deposits in the world. It is located 69 km northeast of Lowestoft, England and about 48 km from the nearest point on the Norfolk coast. The geological structure in which the gas is found is approximately 29 km long and 13 km wide. The water depth is 39 m (125 ft.).

The Leman field extends over 4 leased blocks with 23 licensee companies sharing a portion of the proceeds of the field. Shell/Esso have a 49.72% share of the field, and Amoco and the British Gas Corporation possess a majority of the remaining equity. Shell/Esso are the operators of the western portion of the field and Amoco operates the eastern section.

41

The following types and numbers of platforms have been installed to date in the Leman field: drilling, 9; production, 9; drilling and production combined, 1; compression, 3; terminal, 2; and wellhead satellite, 1. Eleven of these platforms were installed by Shell/Esso and the remainder by Amoco. Details of all 25 platforms are given in Table 5.1.

The gas from the Leman field is processed at facilities in Bacton, England, where both Shell/Esso and Amoco have processing plants. 30-in. pipelines provide a network for transporting the gas from the field to the onshore processing facilities; the gas pipeline network is summarized in Table 5.2.

TABLE 5.1 Description of the platforms in the Leman field.

Platform	Type	Operator	Weights in air (tonnes)		
			Jacket and deck	Modules[a]	Piles
AD	Drilling	Shell/Esso	1912	400[b]	625
AP	Production	Shell/Esso	1235	600	473
ADII	Wellhead satellite	Shell/Esso	1304	50	216
AK	Compression	Shell/Esso	1900	2950	460
BD	Drilling	Shell/Esso	1718	400[b]	814
BP	Production	Shell/Esso	993	650	434
BK	Compression	Shell/Esso	1900	2950	500
BT	Terminal	Shell/Esso	695	300	505
CD	Drilling	Shell/Esso	1745	400[b]	909
CP	Production	Shell/Esso	1061	650	473
D	Drilling/production	Shell/Esso	1642	400[b]	1090
AC	Compression	Amoco	1670	–	800
AD	Drilling	Amoco	956	–	360
AP	Production	Amoco	1014	–	304
BD	Drilling	Amoco	991	–	358
BP	Production	Amoco	1020	–	310
BT	Terminal	Amoco	850[c]	–	400[c]
CD	Drilling	Amoco	1032	–	384
CP	Production	Amoco	1011	–	360
DD	Drilling	Amoco	1011	–	444
DP	Production	Amoco	1171[d]	–	630
ED	Drilling	Amoco	1222	–	637
EP	Production	Amoco	620[c]	–	230
FD	Drilling	Amoco	1015	–	440
FP	Production	Amoco	1174[c,d]	–	680[c]

[a] Includes structure, equipment in modules, and equipment on deck. Data for the weight of modules for Amoco facilities were not available, and estimates for subsequent calculations were made by the author.
[b] Applicable to production phase only, without work over-loads.
[c] Estimates made for jacket, deck, or both, by the operating company.
[d] Estimate made by the author.

42

TABLE 5.2   Gas pipeline network serving the Leman field.

Origin	Destination	Length (km)	Operator
Leman	Bacton	56	Shell/Esso
Leman	Bacton	61	Amoco
Leman	Bacton	64	Amoco–Shell/Esso
Leman	Leman	8	Amoco–Shell/Esso[a]
Indefatigable gas field	Leman	48	Amoco–Shell/Esso

[a] Intra-field link line.

COMPARISON TECHNIQUE

To compare the resources (water, energy, land, manpower, and materials) necessary to produce offshore gas with those required to produce crude oil, an evaluation was performed to help clarify and understand the direct resource requirements for the construction and installation of all offshore gas facilities needed for the Leman field. Next, the direct resource requirements for the operation of these facilities over the production lifetime of the field were developed.

The sum of the direct construction and operating requirements were then compared to similar data developed for 23 offshore oil fields in the U.K. sector of the North Sea, as described in Chapter 2. Three important points should be stressed at the outset: (1) The comparison only includes the direct resource requirements, e.g., those resources physically brought to the construction site or into the North Sea basin. (2) The onshore facilities, such as the Bacton plant or the oil refineries, are not included in the comparison, although the resources necessary to transport the oil or gas to the onshore facility are included. (3) The oil data comprise a composite set developed from 23 different fields; hence, we are comparing a specific gas field, Leman, with a composite set of oil fields.

CONSTRUCTION OF FACILITIES FOR LEMAN FIELD

The major phase of construction activity in the Leman field lasted from April 1966 to August 1968, when production began. However, the drilling of directional production wells and the installation of gas compressors occurred in the subsequent decade, and the major portion of the compressor capacity was installed during the period 1978–1979.

PLATFORMS

A description of the existing platforms has been given in Table 5.1. For the purposes of this study it was assumed that four additional platforms would be installed in the gas field in the period 1980–1988. These additional structures are expected to be 12-well-slot platforms with 10 production wells to be drilled from each [22]. Table 5.3 gives a summarized estimate of the resources necessary to construct and install both the existing platforms and those anticipated in the 1980s.

TABLE 5.3 Total direct resource requirements for platform construction in the Leman field.

Resource (units)	Requirements for				
	Jacket and deck	Modules	Piles	Installation	All construction and installation
Water ($\times$ 10^5 m^3)	–	–	–	–	2.96
Energy					
Electricity ($\times$ 10^5 GJe)	4.47	3.51	–	–	7.98
Motor fuels ($\times$ 10^5 GJ)	–	–	–	12.17	12.17
Process-heat fuels ($\times$ 10^5 GJ)	–	–	–	1.34	1.34
Land (km^2)	–	–	–	–	negligible
Manpower (man-years)	9,860	4,495	–	986	15,341
Materials (tonnes)					
Structural steel	36,163	27,210	14,822	–	78,195

EXPLORATION AND PRODUCTION WELLS
Table 5.4 summarizes the wells drilled to date in the Leman field and those anticipated in the future. The estimated cost in direct resources to drill all of the wells required during the total production lifetime of the Leman field is shown in Table 5.5. It has been assumed that the average depth of each well will be 7600 ft., measured along the bore hole, and that the drilling time will be 45 days for an exploration well and 35 days for a production well.

PIPELINES
The gas pipeline network of the Leman field was described in Table 5.2, and the resources required to construct the network are listed in Table 5.6. It has been assumed in the analysis that the Indefatigable–Leman gas line is only used to provide flexibility in the delivery system and that it is required to transport gas only from the Indefatigable field and not from the Leman field.

SUMMARY OF CONSTRUCTION REQUIREMENTS
Table 5.7 summarizes the resource requirements for past and future construction activities in the Leman field. Marine seismic surveying activity has not been included in the estimate, but, by analogy with similar surveys during the search for oil in the area, its resource requirements are considered to be negligible.

RESOURCES NEEDED TO OPERATE LEMAN FIELD

ENERGY OPERATING REQUIREMENTS
The major resources required to operate and produce gas from an offshore field are energy and labor. A large part of the energy is consumed by the compressors needed to produce the

TABLE 5.11 Summary of the total resources required to develop and operate the Leman gas field and 23 oil fields in the U.K. sector of the North Sea.

Resource (units)	Leman gas field		23 Oil fields	
	Construction	Operation	Construction	Operation
Water ($\times 10^5$ m^3)	30.24	–	287.248	–
Energy				
Electricity ($\times 10^5$ GJe)	13.23	137.00	624.750	–
Motor fuels ($\times 10^5$ GJ)	325.04	856.35	2,851.669	4,040.9
Process-heat fuels ($\times 10^5$ GJ)	3.32	–	34.79	–
Land (km^2)	0.20	–	15.19	–
Manpower (man-years)	22,906	10,539	332,735	85,024
Materials (tonnes)				
Structural steel	162,861	–	2,197,228	–
Reinforcing steel	6,136	–	138,237	–
Prestressed steel	–	–	11,000	–
Pipeline steel	61,124	–	380,203	–
Concrete	–	–	1,630,814	–
Cement	71,185	–	563,410	–
Chemicals	72,903	–	651,285	–
Iron ore	32,686	–	200,219	–
Sand	31,388	–	193,141	–
Asphalt	15,930	–	100,974	–
Ballast	–	–	71,580	–

TABLE 5.12 Comparison of the resource requirements and energy returns for developing and producing North Sea gas and oil.

Resource (units)	Total resources required[a]		Energy return for resources expended	
	Leman gas field (expected return 1.1474 $\times 10^{10}$ GJ)	23 Oil fields (expected return 6.133 $\times 10^{10}$ GJ)	Leman gas field	23 Oil fields
Water ($\times 10^5$ m^3)	30.24	296.35	3,794 GJ/m^3	2,135 GJ/m^3
Energy ($\times 10^5$ GJ)[b]	1,361.4	8,801.61	84.28 GJ/GJ	69.68 GJ/GJ
Land (km^2)	0.20	15.19	Comparison not significant	
Manpower (man-years)	33,445	414,651	3.43 $\times 10^5$ GJ/man-year	1.47 $\times 10^5$ GJ/man-year
Materials (tonnes)	454,213	6,138,091	2.53 $\times 10^4$ GJ/tonne	1.00 $\times 10^4$ GJ/tonne

[a] Including all construction and operational requirements for the lifetime of the field.
[b] Including GJe for construction (assuming 33% efficiency for power production), and GJe for operational use (at an efficiency previously accounted for).

CONCLUSIONS

The main conclusions of this chapter may be summarized as follows:

- The number of units of energy returned per unit of energy expended is 20% greater for developing the Leman gas field than for a set of 23 oil fields in the U.K. sector of the North Sea.
- The number of units of energy returned per unit of water, material, or manpower expended is greater for the Leman field than for the oil fields.

It is therefore apparent that the development of a major gas field in the southern part of the North Sea is a better investment of resources than a similar investment for oil development in the middle or northern parts of the North Sea, where the oil fields of the U.K. sector are located. The comparison also shows that the development of the northern oil fields, which are in deeper water, are more isolated, and experience greater wave heights, requires a significantly greater amount of manpower and material resources. This increased requirement of resources in the north can be directly related to the north's more hazardous environment*.

As mentioned at the beginning of this chapter, the strong bias towards searching for oil in the North Sea basin has been very evident for the last 20 years, due, in part, to the fact that oil is a more flexible commodity. However, it should be kept in mind, as made evident in this chapter, that the development of natural gas fields can, under certain circumstances, return a greater amount of energy than can oil for a similar expenditure of resources during the development and operational stages.

---

*These conclusions lead to an additional question: what would be the results of a similar comparison between a gas field in the *northern* part of the North Sea and the oil fields in the middle and northern parts of the area? Work on this topic continues, and the Elf-Aquitaine Oil Group has provided the author with appropriate data for the Frigg gas field, which is located in the northern part of the North Sea. The results of this new comparison will be published in the near future.

6 NORTH SEA FACILITY DESCRIPTION AND ANALYSIS

The material in this chapter summarizes the direct WELMM (Water, Energy, Land, Manpower, and Materials) requirements for a set of facilities necessary to develop a typical North Sea oil field. A short description of each facility is followed by a WELMM summary of the facility's direct construction or operating requirements. The notes, which close each section, provide more detail about the source and derivation of the summarized WELMM data.

To give the reader some indication of the author's degree of confidence in the data reported, all data have been assigned a "quality" number ranging from 1 to 5, as provided in other similar WELMM studies. The meaning of each quality number is as follows:

Data quality	Definition
1	Very good — highest confidence; error probably $\leqslant 10\%$; data well accepted and verified.
2	Good — reputable and accepted; error probably $\leqslant 25\%$.
3	Fair — error probably $\leqslant 50\%$; validity uncertain due to methods of combining or applying data.
4	Poor — low confidence; error probably $\leqslant 100\%$; validity questionable.
5	Very poor — validity unknown; error probably within or around an order of magnitude.

MARINE SEISMIC SURVEYING VESSEL

Seismic surveying in the North Sea proceeds in two stages: a pre-lease survey which is completed before the purchase of operating rights, and a more detailed survey after the purchase. The surveys are carried out by vessels which house recording instruments and tow a buoyant cable containing hydrophones. Sound waves generated on the vessel are reflected and refracted by the underlying geological strata, and the echoes are picked up by the hydrophones and recorded on magnetic tape. The recorded signals are then used to prepare cross-sectional maps of the sub-surface structure in the area being surveyed. Combinations of cross-sections can be used to build three-dimensional pictures of the underlying strata, thus helping in the identification of geological structures conducive to the accumulation of oil and gas.

The ships used for seismic surveying in the North Sea were not purpose built, but were generally converted from such vessels as seine trawlers by adding more electronic equipment and accommodation facilities. The typical vessel has a total engine power of 1820 h.p., accommodates 30 people, and cruises at 8 knots (14.8 km/hour); the gross weight is approximately 900 tonnes.

MARINE SEISMIC SURVEYING VESSEL:
DIRECT OPERATING RESOURCES

DESCRIPTION	
Facility name	Marine seismic surveying vessel
Characteristics	1820-h.p. engine, 900 tonnes deadweight, accommodates 30 people
Capacity	12,000 miles surveying/year
Annual operating duration	365 days
Lifetime	20 years

RESOURCE REQUIREMENTS				
Resource (units)	Per year	Per mile surveyed	Data quality	Note
Water (m^3)	1355	0.1129	2	N000
Energy (GJ) Motor fuels	85,600	7.1333	2	N001
Land (km^2)	0.02	negligible	3	N002
Manpower (man-years)	70.2	0.0058	2	N003
Materials (tonnes)	negligible	—	—	—

MARINE SEISMIC SURVEYING VESSEL: NOTES

N000   Water requirements for operating the vessel for 1 year are calculated as 19.3 m^3/ man-year $\times$ 70.2 man-years = 1355 m^3; see Appendix for water use and Note N003 for manpower requirements.

N001   Motor fuels needed to operate the 1820 h.p. on board are calculated assuming 25% efficiency and 50% usage; since 1 h.p. = 745.6 J/sec and there are (365 $\times$ 24 $\times$ 3600) seconds per year, the motor-fuel energy requirement is given [23] by:
1820 $\times$ (100/25) $\times$ (50/100) $\times$ (365 $\times$ 24 $\times$ 3600) $\times$ 745.6 = 85,600 GJ

N002   0.02 km^2 (5 acres) required for shore-base operation.

N003   Assuming 1 man-year = 2000 man-hours, the various manpower requirements are 64.8 man-years for vessel operation and 5.4 man-years for shore-base operation, giving a total of 70.2 man-years. Data from the U.K. Department of Energy [13].

NORTH SEA EXPLORATION WELL

The typical exploration well in the U.K. sector of the North Sea is situated north of latitude 56°N, and is drilled by a semi-submersible rig. The rig must be able to withstand fairly extreme weather conditions, including wind speeds of up to 100 knots (185 km/hour) and maximum wave heights of 70 ft. (23 m). The water depth in the area ranges from 120 to 160 m.

The average well is approximately 11,000 ft. (3353 m) long, as measured along the bore-hole because the wells are not normally drilled vertically. For the purposes of this analysis the well is taken to include the casing "string", together with all consumable items needed for drilling, such as chemicals, cement, drill bits, etc. Only part of the drilling conductor and drill pipe are included in the requirements for the exploration well, depending on the average life expectancy of each item.

FIGURE 6.2 The semi-submersible rig *Transworld 58* in operation in the Argyll field. (By courtesy of Hamilton Bros. Oil Co. Ltd.)

NORTH SEA CONCRETE PLATFORM

Concrete platforms are used for the production of crude oil in a number of the fields in the U.K. sector of the North Sea. The typical concrete platform is located north of the $56°N$ parallel in water depths ranging from 120 to 140 m. The platform has a vertical height of 140–200 m (from the mud line to the lowest deck), and is retained in place largely by gravity (since the platform plus ballast is very massive), rather than by the piling process used for steel platforms. The production deck is supported by 3 or 4 legs (or "towers"), and the platform's main building material is concrete (234,000 tonnes), although a certain amount of steel (630 tonnes structural, 11,000 tonnes reinforcing, 1500 tonnes pre-stressed) is also needed, giving a total substructure weight of 247,130 tonnes. In addition, 4860 tonnes of steel plates and girders are required for the deck, together with another 13,965 tonnes of steel for the modules and equipment. The finished platform is protected and reinforced by a steel skirt.

The typical concrete platform has 42 well conductors, and a peak production rate of 6.24×10^6 tonnes of crude oil per year. One important difference from the steel platform is that the concrete platform has 935,000 barrels of internal storage capacity, whereas the steel platform has none.

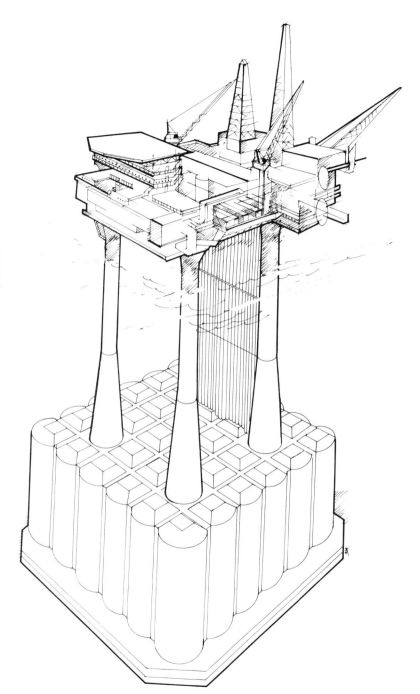

FIGURE 6.3 Artist's impression of an offshore concrete platform.

NORTH SEA CONCRETE PLATFORM:
DIRECT CONSTRUCTION RESOURCES

DESCRIPTION	
Facility name	North Sea concrete platform
Characteristics	Offshore, concrete-gravity platform for crude oil production, operates in water depths 120–140 m, 42 well conductors
Peak production rate	6.24×10^6 tonnes/year
Lifetime production	55.9×10^6 tonnes

RESOURCE REQUIREMENTS				
Resource (units)	For construction and installation	Per tonne produced[a]	Data quality	Note
Water (m^3)	124,900	2.234×10^{-3}	3	N200
Energy				
Electricity (GJe)	15.937×10^5	2.851×10^{-2}	3	N201
Motor fuels (GJ)	2.641×10^5	4.724×10^{-3}	2	N202
Process-heat fuels (GJ)	0.273×10^5	4.883×10^{-4}	3	N203
Land (km^2)	0.276	negligible	2	N204
Manpower (man-years)	5928	1.061×10^{-4}	3	N205
Materials (tonnes)				
Structural steel	22,719	4.064×10^{-4}	1	N206
Reinforcing steel	11,000	1.968×10^{-4}	1	N207
Prestressed steel	1,500	2.683×10^{-5}	1	N207
Concrete	240,506	4.302×10^{-3}	1	N208
Sand and rock	273,876	4.899×10^{-3}	1	N209

[a] Based on total lifetime production capacity.

NORTH SEA CONCRETE PLATFORM: NOTES

N200   Water requirements for construction are derived in two stages: water for human consumption is given by 5484 (man-years) $\times$ 19.3 (m^3/man-year) = 105,841 m^3; that required for concrete is given by 240,506 (tonnes) $\times$ 0.0792 (m^3/tonne) = 19,076 m^3. See the Appendix for more details.

N201   Electricity needed to produce the platform is as follows:

Activity	Electricity needed ($\times 10^5$ GJe)	Reference
Platform construction	3.047	[29], p. 85
Module fabrication	11.34	Macleod [27], p. 16
Deck construction	1.55	Macleod [27], pp. 21, 22
Total	15.937	

N202   Motor-fuel requirements are as follows:

Activity	Motor fuels needed ($\times 10^5$ GJ)	Reference
Transport of materials to site		
Steel	0.186	Hemming [26], p. 58
Cement	0.206	Hemming [26], p. 58
Sand and gravel	0.001	Hemming [26], p. 58
Site excavation	0.082	Macleod [27], p. 13; [29], p. 85
Module installation	1.223	Hemming [26], pp. 54–59
Platform installation	0.943[a]	[30], p. 15
Total	2.641	

[a] Assuming a 6-day tow of 405 km, using a total of 72,000 h.p. of tugs plus 4 assisting vessels each of 5000 h.p.

N203   It is estimated ([41], pp. 29, 30) that approximately 0.273×10^5 GJ is required to lift the modules onto the deck.

N204   Land requirements are estimated as 0.81 km^2 for the construction site plus 0.018 km^2 for an unloading terminal, giving a total of 0.828 km^2. Assuming that 3 platforms are built per site, this total is divided by 3 to give a land requirement of 0.276 km^2 per platform [29].

N205 Manpower requirements for construction are as follows:

Activity	Manpower requirement (man-years)	Reference
Platform and site construction	2840	[29], pp. 84, 85
Deck construction	444	[5–21]
Module fabrication	1985	[31]
Module installation	288	[32], pp. 11–18
Module and tie-in construction, and crewing requirements	354	U.K. Department of Energy [13]
Platform tow-out	17	Bechtel [28], p. 293
Total	5928	

N206 Direct structural steel requirements for constructing and equipping the typical concrete platform are as follows:

Item	Structural steel (tonnes)	Reference
Platform skirt	630	[5, 7, 8]
Deck	4,860	[5, 7, 8]
Modules and equipment	13,965[a]	[5, 7, 8]
Site buildings	131	Vienna Technical University [33]
Site equipment	1,800	[34]
Site storage silos	1,333	[29], p. 85
Total	22,719	

[a] Assuming that 95% of the modules and equipment are high-carbon alloy steel.

N207 Data on reinforcing and prestressed steel were obtained by personal communication with the operating companies [5–21].

N208 Concrete requirements are composed of 234,000 tonnes for platform construction, 5333 tonnes for the graving-dock gates (Macleod [27], p. 13), and 1173 tonnes for building the site (data from *Project Ninian* [34]), a total of 240,506 tonnes.

N209 821,628 tonnes of sand and rock must be excavated and used in the construction of the dry graving dock where the base of the platform is built (data from ref.29, p. 85). Assuming that 3 platform bases are built per graving dock, this total is divided by 3 to give a sand and rock requirement of 273,876 tonnes per platform base.

FIGURE 6.4 The largest concrete platform in the U.K. sector of the North Sea: Ninian Central. (By courtesy of Chevron Petroleum Ltd.)

NORTH SEA STEEL PLATFORM

Steel platforms used in the U.K. sector of the North Sea for crude oil production are fixed-leg structures measuring 140—165 m from the mud line to the lowest deck. The typical platform (located north of the $56°N$ parallel) uses 4—8 legs, and stands in waters from 120 to 140 m deep. Unlike the concrete platform, the steel platform is held in position by an average of 34 piles, driven approximately 52 m into the sea bed; 5700 tonnes of steel are required for the piles. The substructure (or "jacket"), weighing 15,312 tonnes, is fixed to the piles, and it, in turn, supports the deck, modules, and equipment. Typically the deck, which is of steel truss or girder construction, weighs 1372 tonnes, and another 14,450 tonnes must be added to account for the modules and equipment.

The average steel platform has 30 well conductors (slightly less than its concrete counterpart), but has a very similar peak production rate of 6.45×10^6 tonnes of crude oil per year. In marked contrast, however, the steel platform has no provision for internal storage.

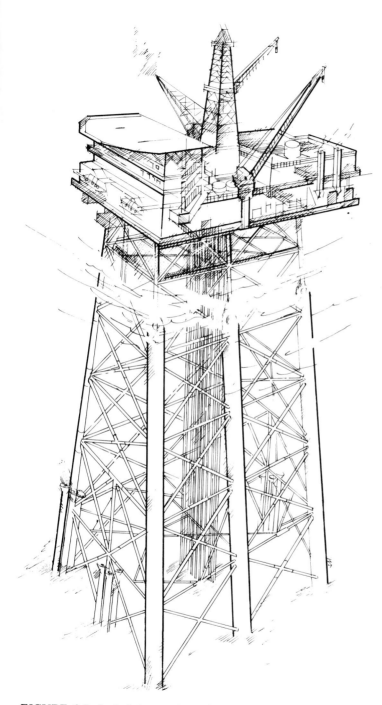

FIGURE 6.5 Artist's impression of an offshore steel platform.

NORTH SEA STEEL PLATFORM: DIRECT CONSTRUCTION RESOURCES

DESCRIPTION	
Facility name	North Sea steel platform
Characteristics	Offshore, fixed-leg steel platform for crude oil production, operates in water depths 120–140 m, has 30 well conductors
Peak production rate	6.45×10^6 tonnes/year
Lifetime production	52.0×10^6 tonnes

RESOURCE REQUIREMENTS				
Resource (units)	For construction and installation	Per tonne produced[a]	Data quality	Note
Water (m³)	143,661	2.763×10^{-3}	3	N300
Energy				
Electricity (GJe)	11.34×10^5	2.181×10^{-2}	3	N301
Motor fuels (GJ)	6.09×10^5	1.171×10^{-2}	2	N302
Process-heat fuels (GJ)	0.82×10^5	1.586×10^{-3}	3	N303
Land (km²)	0.325	negligible	1	N304
Manpower (man-years)	7424	1.428×10^{-4}	3	N305
Materials (tonnes)				
Structural steel	37,027	7.121×10^{-4}	1	N306
Concrete	4,777	0.919×10^{-4}	1	N307
Sand	215,410	4.142×10^{-3}	1	N308

[a]Based on total lifetime production capacity.

NORTH SEA STEEL PLATFORM: NOTES

N300   Water requirements are discussed at greater length in the Appendix and in ref. 35, p. 146. Total human needs are calculated as 7424 (man-years) $\times$ 19.3 (m^3/man-year) = 143,283 m^3; requirements for concrete are 4777 (tonnes) $\times$ 0.0792 (m^3/tonne) = 378 m^3. Thus the overall water requirement is 143,661 m^3.

N301   Electricity required during construction is 6.53 $\times$ 10^5 GJe for the jacket and 4.81 $\times$ 10^5 GJe for the modules and equipment, giving a total of 11.34 $\times$ 10^5 GJe. Data are adapted from Macleod ([27], p. 16), but note that the present author assumes that 95% of the modules and equipment are steel, and that electrical requirements form 64% of the total energy needed, rather than the 50% assumed by Macleod.

N302   According to Macleod [27], the motor-fuel requirements ($\times$ 10^5 GJ) are composed of 0.0643 for site excavation, 1.0768 for platform installation, and 4.95 for module installation (2.82 for tugs, 1.45 for general supply vessels, and 0.68 for barges). This gives a total motor-fuel requirement of 6.09 $\times$ 10^5 GJ.

N303   To drive 34 piles through an average vertical distance of 52 m requires 0.552 $\times$ 10^5 GJ (Macleod [27], pp. 29, 30); to lift 14,450 tonnes of modules and equipment onto the platform from sea level requires 0.273 $\times$ 10^5 GJ [36]. Therefore we arrive at a total "process-heat fuel" requirement of 0.825 $\times$ 10^5 GJ.

N304   The graving dock occupies 1.3 km^2; assuming that 4 platforms are built in the dock, this gives a land requirement of 0.325 km^2 per platform ([37], p. 14).

N305   Manpower requirements for construction and installation are as follows:

Activity	Manpower needed (man-years)	Reference
Platform and site construction	4592	[36]
Module construction	1952	[38]
Platform installation	18	Macleod [27], pp. 23–27
Module installation		
Derrick barge crew	356	Bechtel [28], p. 293
Tugs crew	152	Bechtel [28], p. 293
Construction crew	354	U.K. Department of Energy (personal communication)
Total	7424	

N306 Structural steel requirements for construction are as follows:

Construction of	Structural steel (tonnes)	Reference
Jacket	15,312	[5–21]
Deck	1,372	[5–21]
Modules and equipment	13,727[a]	[5–21]
Piles	5,700	[5–21]
Site buildings	116	[33]
Site cranes	500	Macleod [27], p. 14
Site equipment	300	Macleod [27], p. 14
Total	37,027	

[a] This represents 95% of the total weight of the modules and equipment.

N307 Concrete requirements are composed of 4000 tonnes for site excavation (Macleod [27], p. 13) and 777 tonnes for site buildings [33], giving a total concrete requirement of 4777 tonnes.

N308 215,410 tonnes of sand are assumed to have been excavated from the site and then re-used in the construction of the graving dock. Note that the sand was not transported to the site for construction purposes, and that this total does not include the sand needed for cement mixing ([37], p. 14).

FIGURE 6.6 An example of a North Sea steel platform: Forties FA (Graythorp I). (By courtesy of British Petroleum.)

NORTH SEA PRODUCTION WELL

The typical North Sea production well measures 11,000 ft. (3353 m) along its bore. The well is directionally drilled from the platform and may deviate by as much as 55° from the vertical. Depending on the number of well conductors on the platform, a series of such wells can thus cover a maximum area of 50 hectare at the depth of the oil-bearing strata. The typical well has a production capacity of 183,960 tonnes/ year.

For the purposes of our analysis, the well is taken to include the drilling conductor, casing "string", an allocated portion of the drill pipe, and the blow-out preventor. In addition, all the consumable items needed for drilling, such as chemicals, cement, drill bits, etc., are allocated to the production well; further details are given in Note N406.

It should also be noted that analyses of the WELMM (Water, Energy, Land, Manpower, and Materials) requirements have been carried out for both the construction and the operation of the production well. Construction requirements are dealt with in the table "North Sea Production Well: Direct Construction Resources" and the accompanying Notes N400— 406. Operating requirements are examined in the table "North Sea Production Well: Direct Operating Resources" and Notes N407—409.

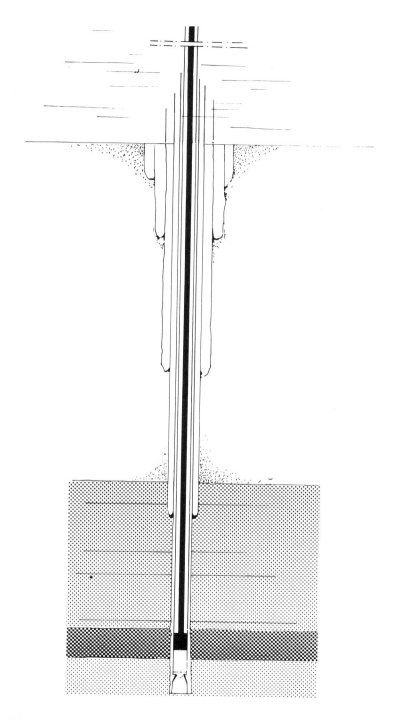

FIGURE 6.7 Schematic diagram of the drilling of an offshore production well.

NORTH SEA PRODUCTION WELL:
DIRECT CONSTRUCTION RESOURCES

DESCRIPTION	
Facility name	North Sea production well
Characteristics	Offshore, 11,000 ft. (3353 m) long measured along bore-hole, including drilling conductor and casing"string"
Construction time	73 days
Capacity	183,960 tonnes/year

RESOURCE REQUIREMENTS				
Resource (units)	For construction and installation	Per tonne produced per year	Data quality	Note
Water (m^3)	20,988	0.1141	4	N400
Energy				
Electricity (GJe)	0.151 $\times$ 10^5	8.208 $\times$ 10^{-2}	3	N401
Motor fuels (GJ)	2.200 $\times$ 10^5	1.196	2	N402
Process-heat fuels (GJ)	0.009 $\times$ 10^5	4.892 $\times$ 10^{-3}	3	N403
Land (km^2)	0.002 (temporary)	1.087 $\times$ 10^{-8}	3	N404
Manpower (man-years)	43.2	2.348 $\times$ 10^{-4}	3	N405
Materials (tonnes)				
Structural steel	883.9	0.0048	2	N406
Cement	406.4	0.0022	2	N406
Chemicals	531.0	0.0029	2	N406

NORTH SEA PRODUCTION WELL: NOTES
(construction resources)

N400 The direct water requirements for constructing the well are composed of 833.7 m^3 fresh water for human needs [43.2 (man-years) $\times$ 19.3 (m^3/man-year)], 154.4 m^3 fresh water for casing cement ([24], p. 62), and 20,000 m^3 treated sea water for drilling mud ([25], p. 80). Thus we arrive at a total requirement of 20,988.1 m^3.

N401 Electrical requirements on board the platform during production drilling are estimated as 10% of total drilling h.p. or 0.151 $\times$ 10^5 GJe.

N402 Motor fuels required to drill and complete the well are calculated as shown in the following tables. The first table, based on the work of Macleod ([27], p. 41), lists the fuel energy required to transport materials to the shore base:

Transport to shore base of	Weight (tonnes)	Distance transported (miles)	Energy required per tonne-mile ($\times 10^6$ J)	Total energy required ($\times 10^5$ GJ)
Chemicals	531.0	3500	0.12	0.00223
Cement	406.4	200	1.20	0.00097
Casing and other steel	869.0	400	1.20	0.00417
Drill bits	14.9	3500	0.12	0.00006
Total				0.00743

The second table, which incorporates the results from the first, extends the survey to cover all motor fuels required in the drilling of the well:

Activity	Fuel-energy requirement ($\times 10^5$ GJ)	Reference
Transporting materials to shore base	0.007	See table above
Operating supply vessels[a]	0.669	Elf-Aquitaine [15]
Operating helicopter	0.019	Hemming [26], p. 10
Drilling[b]	0.903	Macleod [27], p. 41; Hemming [26], p. 27
Operating mud pumps[c]	0.602	Hemming [26], p. 6
Total	2.200	

[a] Assuming 2.5 supply vessels operating per drilling rig and 0.5 vessels available for emergencies.
[b] Assuming a drilling time of 73 days and 4800 drilling h.p. continuously operating at 25% fuel-conversion efficiency.
[c] Assuming mud pumps of a total of 3200 h.p.

N403 Process-heat fuels required for drilling the well conductor for one production well amount to approximately 0.009×10^5 GJ (Macleod [27], p. 40).

N404 A 15-acre (0.061 km^2) shore base is needed for receiving and transferring materials required to the production platform during drilling. Because it is assumed that such a shore base will handle the material requirements for 34 production wells, this leads to a land requirement of 0.44 acres (~ 0.002 km^2) per well.

N405 Direct personnel requirements for developing the production well are as follows:

Activity[a]	Personnel required[b] (man-years)	Reference
Operating supply vessels	11.5	Bechtel [28], p. 281
Operating shore base	6.3	Elf-Aquitaine [15]
Platform drilling		
Drilling	18.8	
Catering	3.5	
Maintenance and services	3.1	
Total	43.2	

[a] 1 man-year = 2000 man-hours.
[b]The personnel required to transport materials to the shore base are considered negligible and are not included in the table.

N406 The direct material requirements for drilling and completing the production well are listed in the following tables. The first table [5] defines the casing "string" requirements for a typical 11,000-ft. North Sea well:

Item	Outside diameter (in.)	Length (ft.)	Weight (lbs./ft.)	Total weight (tonnes)
Conductor	30	700	310	98.5
String	20	1,800	94	76.8
String	13.375	5,500	72	179.7
String	9.625	11,000	47	234.6
Liner	7	1,000	32	14.5
Production string	5.5	11,000	23	114.8
Total				718.9

The second table, which incorporates the results of the first, extends the analysis to include all the materials required [5] to complete the well:

Item	Material weight (tonnes)		
	Steel	Cement	Chemicals
Drill bits[a]	14.9		
Wire string [b]	15.7		
Cement		406.4	
Drilling mud			531.0
Drill collars[c]	1.5		
Casing[d]	718.9		
Blow-out preventor	130.0		
Drill pipe[e]	2.9		
Total	883.9	406.4	531.0

[a] 7–10 drill bits are employed per well.
[b] 50–60 ft. of wire string are consumed during 24 hours drilling.
[c] Assuming one drill collar used per well.
[d] Derived from the first table in this Note.
[e] Assuming the lifetime of the drill pipe to be 7.5 years, the annual number of wells drilled to be 4.5, and the weight of 5-in. pipe to be 19.5 lb./ft.

NORTH SEA PRODUCTION WELL: DIRECT OPERATING RESOURCES

DESCRIPTION	
Facility name	North Sea production well
Characteristics	Offshore, 11,000 ft. (3353 m) long measured along bore-hole, including drilling conductor and casing "string"
Capacity	183,960 tonnes/year
Output	183,960 tonnes/year
Annual operating duration	365 days
Lifetime	40 years

RESOURCE REQUIREMENTS				
Resource (units)	Per year	Per tonne produced per year	Data quality	Note
Water (m^3)				
Fresh water	258	0.0014	2	N407
Sea water	821,332	4.4647	3	N407
Energy (GJ)				
Motor fuels	0.30107×10^5	0.1637	3	N408
Land (km^2)	negligible	—	—	—
Manpower (man-years)	7.75	4.2128×10^{-5}	3	N409
Materials (tonnes)	negligible	—	—	—

NORTH SEA PRODUCTION WELL: NOTES
(operating resources)

N407 Assuming that water injection is being used in the field, the annual water requirements for operating the well are as follows: 258 m^3 fresh water for human needs, 330,695 m^3 treated sea water for cooling, and 490,637 m^3 treated sea water for water injection.

Data were obtained from Shell Oil Ltd. and other North Sea operating companies [5–21].

N408 The motor fuels required for one year's production of crude oil are as follows:

Activity	Motor-fuel energy required ($\times 10^5$ GJ/year)	Reference
Crude oil production[a]	0.21856	Macleod [27], p. 48
Operating supply vessels[b]	0.08151	Macleod [27], p. 49
Operating helicopter[c]	0.00100	Macleod [27], p. 49
Operating shore base	negligible	Hemming [26], p. 41
Total	0.30107	

[a] Assuming an output of 183,960 tonnes/year, and excluding any energy required for water injection.

[b] Assuming that 5 supply vessels service a major field, i.e., that there are more than 100 wells in the field.

[c] Assuming that 15 return helicopter trips, each trip being a total of 300 miles long, are made to the production platform per week.

N409 The manpower required to operate the well for one year is as follows:

Activity	Personnel requirements (man-years)	Reference
Production on platform	1.59	U.K. Department of Energy [13]
Maintenance	2.30	U.K. Department of Energy [13]
Operating supply vessels	2.01	Bechtel [28], p. 293
Operating helicopter	0.17	Macleod [27], p. 49
Operating shore base	1.68	[5–21]
Total	7.75	

OFFSHORE OIL AND GAS PIPELINES

Various systems of pipelines are used in the North Sea to link the different offshore facilities and to transport the crude oil and gas from the fields to the onshore terminals. Intra-field pipelines, typically of 4.5–24-in. outside diameter, transmit oil and gas from subsea wells to production platforms, and from production platforms to offshore loading terminals (single-point or single-buoy moorings), to remote flare vents, and to other production platforms. Networks of inter-field pipelines, typically of 16–36-in. outside diameter, carry the oil or gas from one field to another and finally to the onshore terminal facilities.

The pipelines are placed in position by a laying barge, and are buried beneath the mud line to prevent damage from currents, waves, storms, and anchors. The inter-field pipelines are coated with asphalt and concrete, although this is not considered necessary for the smaller pipes. It is assumed that all the inter-field pipelines are more than 90 miles long.

It should be noted that analyses of the WELMM (Water, Energy, Land, Manpower, and Materials) requirements have been carried out for both the construction and the operation of pipelines. Construction requirements are dealt with in the table "Offshore Oil and Gas Pipelines: Direct Construction Resources" and Notes N500–512; the format of the table differs slightly from that used elsewhere in this chapter because pipelines of a number of different diameters are analyzed. Operating requirements are examined in the table "Offshore Oil and Gas Pipelines: Direct Operating Resources" and Notes N513–515.

FIGURE 6.8 The semi-submersible pipe-laying barge *Semac I*. (By courtesy of Shell U.K. Ltd.)

OFFSHORE OIL AND GAS PIPELINES:
DIRECT CONSTRUCTION RESOURCES

DESCRIPTION	
Facility name	Offshore crude oil pipeline
Characteristics	Located in the North Sea, coated pipes buried in the sea bed
Size	Various, outside diameters ranging from 4.5 in. to 36 in.

WATER REQUIREMENTS (m^3); (data quality 3)		
Outside diameter of pipe (in.)	*For construction, installation, and burial of 1 mile; see Note N500*	
	Water for concrete coating	*Water for human needs*
4.5	—	—
6.0	— coating not required	— not available, due to inadequate data and scaling problems
10.0	—	—
16.0	18	237
20.0	31	296
24.0	46	356
30.0	56	444
32.0	59	474
36.0	66	533

ENERGY REQUIREMENTS; (data quality 3)			
Outside diameter of pipe (in.)	*For construction, installation, and burial of 1 mile*		
	Electricity ($\times 10^5$ GJe); see Note N501	*Motor fuels ($\times 10^5$ GJ); see Notes N502–504*	*Process-heat fuels ($\times 10^5$ GJ); see Note N505*
4.5	0.0067	0.0383	0.0003
6.0	0.0089	0.0514	0.0005
10.0	0.0148	0.0861	0.0007
16.0	0.0237	0.1393	0.0013
20.0	0.0297	0.1748	0.0017
24.0	0.0356	0.2120	0.0021
30.0	0.0445	0.2665	0.0026
32.0	0.0475	0.2850	0.0027
36.0	0.0534	0.3205	0.0030

LAND REQUIREMENTS (km^2)			
For onshore storage	*Per mile of pipe*	*Data quality*	*Note*
0.165	0.0014	3	N506

MANPOWER REQUIREMENTS (man-years); (data quality 3)

Outside diameter of pipe (in.)	For construction, installation, and burial of 1 mile	
	Construction and installation; see Note N507	Burial; see Note N508
4.5	— ⎫ not available, due to	— ⎫ not available, due to
6.0	— ⎬ inadequate data	— ⎬ inadequate data and
10.0	— ⎭ and scaling problems	— ⎭ scaling problems
16.0	9.67	2.62
20.0	12.09	3.27
24.0	14.51	3.92
30.0	18.13	4.90
32.0	19.34	5.23
36.0	21.76	5.88

MATERIAL REQUIREMENTS (tonnes); (data quality 3)

Outside diameter of pipe (in.)	For construction of 1 mile					
	Rolled steel; see Note N509	Reinforcing steel; see Note N510	Concrete; see Note N511	Iron ore; see Note N511	Sand; see Note N511	Asphalt coating; see Note N512
4.5	21	—	—	—	—	16
6.0	44	—	—	—	—	25
10.0	99	—	—	—	—	40
16.0	180	18	54	91	88	66
20.0	250	25	90	152	146	91
24.0	338	34	134	227	219	109
30.0	518	52	163	277	266	135
32.0	602	60	173	293	282	144
36.0	679	68	192	326	313	161

OFFSHORE OIL AND GAS PIPELINES: NOTES
(construction resources)

N500   Water requirements for constructing, laying, and burying 1 mile of pipeline are based on the values (see Appendix) 19.3 m^3/man-year for human needs and 0.0793 m^3/tonne for concrete coating.

N501 5.607×10^5 GJe of electrical energy is required for welding a pipeline of outside diameter 32 in. and length 118 miles (Macleod [27]). We assume that the energy required is linearly dependent on the outside diameter, D, of the pipe, and thus arrive at the formula:
Electrical energy required = 148.49 D GJe/mile

N502   The motor-fuel energy needed to construct, lay, and bury 1 mile of pipeline is derived from Macleod's study ([27], pp. 35–39) of a 32-in. pipeline 118 miles long; Macleod's results are as follows:

Operation of	Energy required for 118 miles of	
	Pipe laying ($\times 10^5$ GJ)	Pipe burying ($\times 10^5$ GJ)
Pipe carrier vessels	2.910	—
Supply vessels	1.450	0.091
Tugs	10.000	—
Shore base	0.003	negligible
Helicopter	0.007	0.003
Burying barge	—	13.140
Service vessel	—	4.260
Total	14.370	17.494

From the results above, and assuming that the energy required is linearly dependent on the outside diameter , D, of the pipe, the following relationships were derived:
Motor-fuel energy for pipe laying = 380.56 D GJ/mile
Motor-fuel energy for pipe burying = 463.28 D GJ/mile
Using these relationships, the detailed energy requirements given in the table overleaf were calculated.

Outside diameter of pipe (in.)	Energy required for 1 mile of	
	Pipe laying ($\times 10^5$ GJ)	Pipe burying ($\times 10^5$ GJ)
4.5	0.0171	0.0208
6.0	0.0228	0.0278
10.0	0.0381	0.0463
16.0	0.0609	0.0741
20.0	0.0761	0.0926
24.0	0.0913	0.1111
30.0	0.1142	0.1389
32.0	0.1218	0.1482
36.0	0.1370	0.1667

Motor-fuel energy requirements for the concrete coating and the transport of materials are given in Notes N503 and N504, respectively.

N503 The motor-fuel energy required to coat the pipeline with concrete is assumed (Peckham [39]) to be 10% of the process-heat fuel energy for the material. As the process-heat fuel energy for concrete is 2.55 GJ/tonne, we arrive at the following values for each diameter of pipe:

Outside diameter of pipe (in.)	Energy required to coat 1 mile with concrete ($\times 10^5$ GJ)
4.5	— ⎫
6.0	— ⎬ coating not required
10.0	— ⎭
16.0	0.0006
20.0	0.0010
24.0	0.0015
30.0	0.0018
32.0	0.0019
36.0	0.0021

Motor-fuel energy requirements for pipe laying and burying are given in Note N502 and those for transport of materials in Note N504.

N504 Motor fuels required to transport materials to the offshore location have been studied by Peckham [39]. For the steel pipes, two cases are examined:

1. The steel pipes are manufactured in Japan and transported by cargo vessel to the North Sea area at an energy cost of 0.12 MJ/tonne-mile; a transport distance of 13,000 miles is assumed.

2. The steel pipes are manufactured in the United Kingdom and transported by road at an energy cost of 1.20 MJ/tonne-mile; a transport distance of 400 miles is assumed.

In both cases the coating materials, iron ore, reinforcing steel, and asphalt are assumed to be transported by road within the United Kingdom or Western Europe (an average distance of 400 miles) at an energy cost of 1.2 MJ/tonne-mile. Sand is assumed to be transported only a small distance at a negligible energy cost. Peckham's results for both cases are given in the following table, but for the purposes of the present analysis we have assumed that all steel pipes used come from Japan.

Outside diameter of pipe (in.)	Energy required to transport materials 1 mile ($\times 10^5$ GJ)				
	Coating materials, etc., from U.K.	Steel pipe from		Total, steel pipe from	
		U.K.	Japan	U.K.	Japan
4.5	0.00008	0.00010	0.00033	0.00018	0.00041
6.0	0.00012	0.00021	0.00069	0.00033	0.00081
10.0	0.00019	0.00048	0.00154	0.00067	0.00173
16.0	0.00126	0.00086	0.00280	0.00212	0.00366
20.0	0.00199	0.00120	0.00390	0.00319	0.00510
24.0	0.00283	0.00162	0.00527	0.00445	0.00810
30.0	0.00350	0.00249	0.00808	0.00599	0.01158
32.0	0.00374	0.00289	0.00939	0.00663	0.01313
36.0	0.00417	0.00326	0.01059	0.00743	0.01476

Motor-fuel energy requirements for pipe laying and burying, and for the concrete coating, are given in Notes N502 and N503, respectively.

N505 Peckham [39] estimates that the process-heat fuel energy required for the asphalt coating is 10% of the total energy cost of the material (18.9 GJ/tonne).

N506 The temporary land requirements are 15.65 acres (pipe storage), 15.65 acres (space between pipe storage), and 10.0 acres (buildings, terminals, etc.), making a total of 41.3 acres, or 0.165 km². The original calculations were made for pipes of 32-in. outside diameter but we have also assumed them to be valid for larger- and smaller-diameter pipes.

N507 To investigate the manpower requirements for constructing and laying pipelines of various diameters a detailed study was made of an offshore pipeline of 32-in. outside diameter, assumed to be at least 100 miles long and laid in water depths of up to 140 m. Because the circumference of the pipe (and therefore its outside surface area) vary linearly with the outside diameter, it was assumed that the manpower requirements for welding (proportional to total circumference) and coating (proportional to total surface area) also depend linearly on the outside diameter. Therefore the total manpower requirements for constructing and laying the 32-in. pipe were linearly scaled up or down to provide data for pipelines of other dimensions. The detailed requirements for the 32-in. pipe are as follows:

Operation of	Manpower required to construct and lay 1 mile (man-years)	Reference
Coating equipment	0.51	
Laying barge	9.87	Macleod [27], p. 36
Supply vessels	1.74	Macleod [27], p. 35
Pipeline carriers	1.74	Macleod [27], p. 35
Helicopter	0.05	Hemming [26], p. 36
Tugs	1.74	Macleod [27], p. 35
On-shore supply base	3.69	
Total	19.34	

Manpower requirements for pipe burying are given in Note N508.

N508 The manpower requirements for the burial of pipelines were again based on a study of a 32-in. outside diameter pipeline, at least 100 miles long and buried in water depths of up to 140 m, as discussed in Note N507. It was assumed that the manpower requirements vary linearly with the outside diameter of the pipe, and the results for the 32-in. pipe were linearly scaled up or down to generate data for pipes of different dimensions. The detailed requirements for the 32-in. pipe are as follows:

Operation of	Manpower required for burying 1 mile (man-years)	Reference
Burying barge	3.47	Macleod [27], p. 38
Tugs	0.64	Macleod [27], p. 37
Survey vessel	0.31	Macleod [27], p. 37
Supply vessel	0.31	Macleod [27], p. 37
On-shore supply base	0.50	
Total	5.23	

Manpower requirements for pipe construction and laying are given in Note N507.

N509 The weight of rolled steel needed to construct the pipeline is based on two variable parameters, the outside diameter, D, and the thickness of the wall, t_w. Using the conversion factors 63,360 in. = 1 mile, 1728 in.^{3} = 1 ft.^{3}, and 2204 lb. = 1 tonne, together with a steel density of 491 lb./ft.^{3}, leads to the following expression for the weight (tonnes) of steel needed for 1 mile of pipe:

$$\pi(D - t_w)(t_w)(63,360/1728)(491/2204) \text{ tonnes/mile}.$$

N510 Based on the amount of reinforcing steel needed to construct the Forties pipeline (Macleod [27], p. 34), we assumed the reinforcing steel requirement to be 10% of the weight of the rolled steel.

N511 The concrete coating of the offshore pipeline is made from a mixture of cement, iron ore, and heavy aggregates. Using the conversion factors given in Note N510, defining t_a and t_c as the thickness of the asphalt and concrete coatings, respectively, and assuming a concrete density of 160 lb./ft.^{3}, we arrive at the following formula for the weight (tonnes) of concrete coating needed for 1 mile of pipe:

$$\pi(D + 2t_a + t_c)(t_c)(63,360/1728)(160/2204) \text{ tonnes/mile}.$$

Based on values from Bredero-Price B.V. [16], we assumed the concrete to contain 39.2% iron ore, 37.7% sand, and 23.1% cement: these values were later used to calculate the total requirement for each material.

N512 The weights of asphalt coating are based upon data provided by Bredero-Price B.V. [16].

OFFSHORE OIL AND GAS PIPELINES:
DIRECT OPERATING RESOURCES

DESCRIPTION	
Facility name	Offshore oil and gas pipelines
Characteristics	Located in the North Sea, coated pipes buried in the sea bed
Size	Various, outside diameters ranging from 16 in. to 36 in.
Annual operating duration	365 days
Lifetime	40 years

RESOURCE REQUIREMENTS			
Resource (units)	Per tonne of crude oil transported	Data quality	Note
Water (m^3)			
Fresh water	1.015×10^{-3}	2	N513
Treated sea water	1.955	3	N513
Energy (GJ)			
Motor fuels	1.262×10^{-1}	3	N514
Land (km^2)	negligible	—	—
Manpower (man-years)	6.39×10^{-6}	3	N515
Materials (tonnes)	negligible	—	—

N513 Based on information supplied by Shell Oil Ltd. and other North Sea operating companies [5–21], the water required to transfer 1 tonne of crude oil to shore is 1.0157×10^{-3} m^3 fresh water (for human needs, cleaning, etc.) and 1.9554 m^3 treated sea water (for cooling).

N514 The motor-fuel energy required to transfer 1 tonne of crude oil to shore is as follows:

Operation of	Motor-fuel energy required (GJ/tonne)	Reference
Pumping equipment[a]	9.66×10^{-2}	Macleod [27], p. 48
Supply vessels [b]	2.9219×10^{-2}	Macleod [27], p. 49
Helicopter	3.7738×10^{-4}	Macleod [27], p. 49
Shore base	0[c]	
Total	1.262×10^{-1}	

[a] Assuming that the pipeline is 108 miles long (the average length of the existing and anticipated major crude oil pipelines in the North Sea).

[b] Assumes 5 supply vessels, of which 44.8% are directly or indirectly assigned to pipeline operations.

[c] Shore-base activities are considered as a part of the operation of the onshore terminal facility, and are therefore excluded here.

N515 Manpower requirements for transporting 1 tonne of crude oil to shore via an offshore pipeline (outside diameter 16–36 in.) are as follows:

Operation of	Manpower required (man-years/tonne)	Reference
Pumping equipment	2.28×10^{-6}	U.K. Department of Energy [13]
Maintenance work	2.19×10^{-6}	U.K. Department of Energy [13]
Supply vessels	1.92×10^{-6}	Bechtel [28], p. 281
Shore base	0[a]	
Total	6.39×10^{-6}	

[a] Shore-base personnel are considered as part of the requirements of the onshore terminal facility, and are therefore excluded here.

SINGLE-POINT MOORING (SPM)

The single-point mooring system (SPM) is used to load crude oil into tankers at the site of the offshore field. A pylon or "tower" is anchored to the sea bed by a 1400-tonne steel and concrete base; steel blades on the bottom of the base sink into the sea bed to ensure firm positioning. The tower supports a long, swivel-mounted arm, which carries above-water tanker-loading equipment. The tanker moors to the SPM and the head of the SPM rotates, thus allowing the vessel to orient itself in the line of least resistance to the wind, waves, and currents.

Crude oil is transported via a submarine pipeline from the production platform to the base of the SPM. The oil is then transferred to the tanker, at an average rate of 40,000 barrels/hour, using a 16-in. flexible hose from the steel boom of the SPM.

For the purposes of our analysis, the SPM includes all the materials needed for fabrication, together with any necessary ballast. It is also assumed that the SPM is transported 650 miles (1046 km) to its field location using tugs and barges. The pumping equipment needed to transfer the crude oil to the tanker is considered to be part of the production platform facility, and the 1-mile (1.6-km) submarine pipeline is treated as a separate facility.

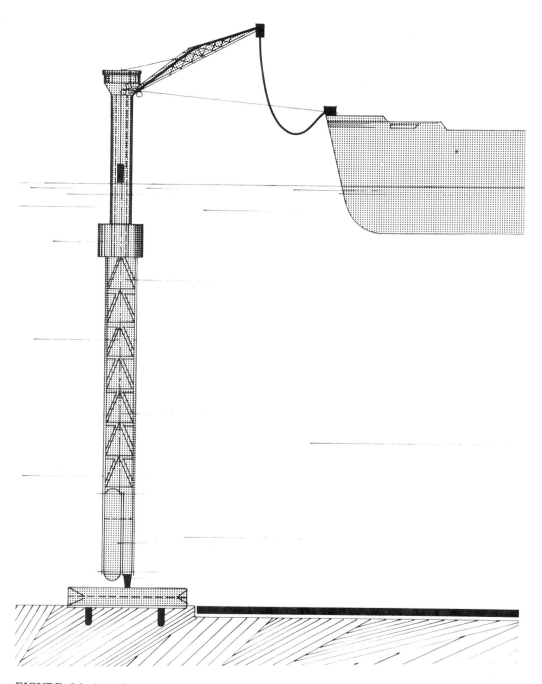

FIGURE 6.9 Artist's impression of a Single-Point Mooring (SPM) offshore loading facility.

SINGLE-POINT MOORING (SPM): DIRECT CONSTRUCTION RESOURCES

DESCRIPTION	
Facility name	Single-point mooring (SPM)
Characteristics	Facility for loading crude oil into tankers in a North Sea field location
Capacity	40,000 barrels/hour

RESOURCE REQUIREMENTS				
Resource (units)	For construction and installation	Per barrel loaded per hour	Data quality	Note
Water (m^3)	1801	4.5×10^{-2}	3	N600
Energy				
Electricity (GJe)	0.117×10^5	2.925×10^{-1}	3	N601
Motor fuels (GJ)	0.052×10^5	1.300×10^{-1}	3	N602
Land (km^2)	negligible	—	—	N603
Manpower (man-years)	92	2.3×10^{-3}	3	N604
Materials (tonnes)				
Structural steel	978.2	2.445×10^{-2}	2	N605
Concrete	324.0	8.100×10^{-3}	2	N606

SINGLE-POINT MOORING (SPM): NOTES

N600   Using the values given in the Appendix, the water required for human needs is 92 (man-years) $\times$ 19.3 (m^3/man-year) = 1776 m^3, and the amount needed for concrete is 324 (tonnes) $\times$ 0.0793 (m^3/tonne) = 25 m^3. Therefore we arrive at a total direct nominal requirement of 1801 m^3.

N601   Electrical requirements for the fabrication of the SPM are calculated as 0.1168 $\times$ 10^5 GJe, based on Hemming's calculation [26] that 25% of the total indirect energy (gross energy requirement) of the materials is used to fabricate the finished structural-steel product.

N602   Motor fuels required to transport the SPM from its fabrication site to the testing site, and then to the offshore field for installation, are calculated as follows. It is assumed that the SPM will be placed on a barge and towed for 650 miles (1046 km) by a 5000-h.p. tug operating at 70% power loading. Since the speed of transport is assumed to be 5 knots (9.26 km/hour), 4.7 days will be spent in reaching the field, and a further 1 day is assumed necessary for installation, giving an overall time of 5.7 days. The tug uses fuel at a rate of 25 tonnes/day, so the total fuel required is 25 $\times$ 5.7 $\times$ 70% (power loading) = 99.75 tonnes. Using the conversion factors 1 tonne fuel = 1.455 $\times$ 10^4 kW-hour = 5.238 $\times$ 10^{10} J, we arrive at a total motor-fuel requirement of 0.05224 $\times$ 10^5 GJ.
Data are taken from Mortimer [40], pp. 4–8.

N603   The land required to construct an SPM is considered to be negligible. It should be noted that, because the tanker may swing round through 360° during loading (depending on weather conditions), a circular area of radius 1 mile (1.6 km) around the SPM is prohibited to other North Sea traffic while loading is in progress.

N604   The personnel requirements for fabrication, testing, and installation of the SPM are estimated as 92 man-years. Data were difficult to obtain, but the calculations were based on the monetary value of the SPM [38] and on the work of Bechtel ([28], p. 383) dealing with the construction requirements for an offshore oil-import facility.

N605   The direct steel requirements for constructing the base and tower of a typical SPM are 122.8 tonnes (steel forgings), 61.4 tonnes (iron/steel castings), and 794.0 tonnes (structural steel), making a total requirement of 978.2 tonnes. All values were taken from Bechtel [28].

N606   Concrete requirements for the base of the tower are 324.0 tonnes [5–21].

FLARE VENT

Many production platforms in the North Sea are equipped with a flare vent facility. This is used to burn off excess amounts of gas at a safe distance from the platform, during production start-ups and maintenance periods, and also to allow for the rapid relief of high pressures which may build up in production units during emergencies. The facility consists of a base which supports a triangular-section, steel-lattice tower, and a steel bridge which links the flare tower to the production platform.

When in operation, the excess gas is carried by pipe along the connecting bridge from the platform to the flare vent; the vent, which is located at the extreme (flare-tower) end of the pipe, is equipped with a pilot burner which ignites the gas as it leaves the vent.

FIGURE 6.10 The flare vent facility attached to Beryl A platform. (By courtesy of Mobil Oil Ltd.)

FLARE VENT: DIRECT CONSTRUCTION RESOURCES

DESCRIPTION	
Facility name	Flare vent
Characteristics	For safe discharge of excess gas during production start-up, maintenance, or emergency; supported by triangular-section steel tower and connected to production platform via a pipeline running across a steel bridge

RESOURCE REQUIREMENTS			
Resource *(units)*	*For construction* *and installation*	*Data* *quality*	*Note*
Water (m^3)	2927	2	N700
Energy			
Electricity (GJe)	0.313 × 10^5	3	N701
Motor fuels (GJ)	0.407 × 10^5	3	N702
Process-heat fuels (GJ)	0.003 × 10^5	2	N703
Land (km^2)	negligible	—	N704
Manpower (man-years)	90	3	N705
Materials (tonnes)			
Structural steel	2,250	1	N706
Concrete	15,000	1	N707

FLARE VENT: NOTES

N700 Using the information given in the Appendix, the direct nominal water requirements for constructing the flare vent are calculated as follows: total human needs are 90 (man-years) $\times$ 19.3 (m^3/man-years) = 1737 m^3; total needs for concrete are 15,000 (tonnes) $\times$ 0.0793 (m^3/tonne) = 1190 m^3. Thus we arrive at a total water requirement of 2927 m^3.

N701 Electrical requirements for the construction of the flare vent are calculated as 0.313 $\times$ 10^5 GJe, based on Hemmings's calculation [26] that 25% of the total indirect energy (gross energy requirement) of the materials is used to fabricate the finished structural-steel product.

N702 Motor fuels required in the construction and installation of the facility are as follows:

Activity	Motor-fuel requirement ($\times$ 10^5 GJ)	Reference
Transport of		
Materials to fabrication site	0.017	Hemming [26], p. 58
Bridge to offshore site	0.052	Hemming [26], p. 47
Tower to offshore site	0.052	Hemming [26], p. 47
Base to offshore site	0.207	Macleod [27], pp. 26, 27
Installation of flare	0.079	[32], p. 19
Total	0.407	

N703 The process-heat fuel required to assemble the facility is 0.003 $\times$ 10^5 GJ. Data taken from Macleod [27], p. 31 and [32], p. 19.

N704 Land requirements are considered to be negligible, because no permanent site has been developed specifically for the construction of flare vents.

N705 The personnel requirement of 90 man-years includes the stages of fabrication, assembly, testing, and installation of the facility. Calculations are based on the costs (in 1973) of fabricating and installing the facility (US $ 1.685 $\times$ 10^6), but exclude the cost of materials (US $ 1.870 $\times$ 10^6).
Data are taken from an internal Elf-Aquitaine paper, and from refs. 15 and 38.

N706 The direct steel requirements for a typical flare vent are composed of 1050 tonnes for the bridge and 1200 tonnes for the tower, giving a total requirement of 2250 tonnes ([32], p. 19).

N707 15,000 tonnes of concrete are required for the base of the flare tower. It should be noted that the concrete "gravity" base can be replaced by a piled construction if the sea-bed conditions are appropriate for pile driving; however, the latter procedure is more difficult, and is therefore not widely used.

ARGYLL FIELD (continued)

RESERVES	
Crude oil	4.5×10^6 tonnes
Gas	Gas/oil ratios: 150 scf/bbl, 300 scf/bbl

TRANSWORLD 58 PLATFORM

GENERAL	
Name	Transworld 58
Installation date	March 1975
Fabrication site	Rotterdam, the Netherlands
Modification company	Converted by Wilson-Walton, Teesside, England
Modification site	Teesside, England
Type of jacket	Mobile rig, semi-submersible
Number of legs	0 (semi-submersible)
Standard well conductors	0
Subsea well conductors	8
Production capacity	Initial, 40,000 bbl/day; potential, 60,000 bbl/day
Storage capacity	0
SUBSTRUCTURE	
Weight structural steel for semi-submersible	4500 tonnes
Total weight semi-submersible (including deck, modules, and equipment)	6800 tonnes
SUPERSTRUCTURE	
Weight of modules and equipment	2300 tonnes

ARGYLL ANCILLARY FACILITIES

OFFSHORE INTRA-FIELD PIPELINES		
Function	*Outside diameter (in.)*	*Length (km)*
Oil: gathering system—subsea wells	4.5	2.25
Transworld 58—"SBM" (see below)	10.75	2.28
FIELD TERMINAL LOADING SYSTEM		
Terminal construction	Single-point Buoy Mooring (SBM)	
Storage capacity	0	
TANKERS		
Number	2	
Weight	55,000 tonnes deadweight each	

AUK

The Auk field was discovered in February 1971 and has been developed by Shell. With reserves of 8 million tonnes it is one of the smaller North Sea fields, and production problems have been encountered due to rising water levels in the oil-bearing formation. A single steel platform installed in July 1974 has been used for development and production, and the peak production rate of 48,000 barrels/day was reached in 1977. As expected, output has since declined, and it will probably average 20,000 barrels/day over the period 1979/1980. Oil from the field is transported to shore by tankers which are loaded at an Exposed-location Single Buoy Mooring (ESBM) facility. Three new platform wells were drilled during 1979.

FIGURE 7.2 Auk production platform. (By courtesy of Shell U.K. Ltd.)

AUK FIELD

GENERAL	
Name	Auk
Location	Block 30/16
Operator	Shell (UK) Ltd.
Company interest	Shell (UK) Ltd. (50%); Esso Petroleum Co. Ltd. (50%)
Discovery date	February 1971
Production date	February 1976
Peak production rate	2.3×10^6 tonnes/year in 1977
API gravity of crude oil	$37.15°$
Number of platforms	1 (Auk)

ENVIRONMENT	
Water depth	84 m
Geological structure	Permian/Zechstein/Rotliegendes
Dimension of geological structure	30 km^2

DISCOVERY DRILLING	
Dry wells before discovery well	1
Appraisal wells after discovery well (including any dry wells)	3
Total wells to determine viability	5 (including discovery well)

PRODUCTION DRILLING	
Total wells anticipated (including reinjection wells)	9
Average expected depth	2286 m

RESERVES	
Crude oil	8×10^6 tonnes

AUK PLATFORM

GENERAL	
Name	Auk
Installation date	July 1974
Fabricating company	Redpath, Dorman and Long (North Sea) Ltd.
Fabrication site	Methil, Scotland
Building time (contract to installation)	26 months
Type of jacket	Steel
Number of legs	8
Vertical height (from mud line to lowest deck)	102.9 m
Standard well conductors	12
Subsea well conductors	0
Production capacity	80,000 bbl/day
Storage capacity	0
SUBSTRUCTURE	
Piles driven	20
Average depth driven	30 m
Total weight steel for piles	1960 tonnes
Weight structural steel for jacket	3360 tonnes
Total weight jacket (excluding deck, modules, and equipment)	3360 tonnes
SUPERSTRUCTURE	
Type of deck	Steel, truss deck
Weight of deck	450 tonnes
Weight of modules and equipment	5000 tonnes

AUK ANCILLARY FACILITIES

OFFSHORE INTRA-FIELD PIPELINES		
Function	*Outside diameter (in.)*	*Length (km)*
Oil: Auk platform—"ELSBM" (see below)	10	1.98

FIELD TERMINAL LOADING SYSTEM	
Terminal construction	Exposed Location Single Buoy Mooring (ELSBM)
Storage capacity	0
Overall height	73.76 m
Weight of steel	1500 tonnes
Weight of ballast	1450 tonnes
Total weight	2950 tonnes (excluding anchor and chain)
Weight of anchor	120 tonnes
Weight of chain	403 tonnes

TANKERS	
Number	2
Weight	41,880 tonnes deadweight each

BEATRICE

Beatrice was discovered in September 1976 and is one of the smaller North Sea fields. It is very close ($\sim$ 20 km) to the shore and the reservoir is located beneath shallow water ($\sim$ 45 m); these factors have considerably reduced development costs, thereby enhancing the value of the reserves, which are estimated as 21 million tonnes. The field was originally to be developed by Mesa U.K., but BNOC took over as the operating company in 1979. Two centrally located twin platforms will be used to drill and produce the oil for the larger part of the field, and a jack-up rig (*Zapata Nordic*) at the north-east end of the structure will be employed as a satellite production facility. Production is expected to begin in 1981 and the oil will be transported by pipeline to Nigg Bay.

FIGURE 7.3 Beatrice drilling platform. (By courtesy of BNOC.)

BEATRICE FIELD

GENERAL	
Name	Beatrice
Location	Block 11/30
Operator	British National Oil Corporation (BNOC)
Company interest	BNOC (28%); Kerr McGee Oil (UK) Ltd. (15%); Deminex (London) (22%); British Petroleum Ltd. (15%); Hunt Oil (UK) Ltd. (10%)
Discovery date	August 1976
Production date	Expected mid-to-late 1981
Peak production rate	3.9×10^6 tonnes/year
API gravity of crude oil	$38.4°$
Number of platforms	3 (Beatrice Drilling Platform; Beatrice Production Platform; Zapata Nordic)

ENVIRONMENT	
Water depth	45 m
Geological structure	Middle Jurassic
Dimension of geological structure	17.2 km^2

DISCOVERY DRILLING	
Total wells to determine viability	4

PRODUCTION DRILLING	
Total wells anticipated (including reinjection wells)	37 (22 production on main jacket; 5 production on jack-up; 10 water injection, of which 7 on main jacket and 3 on jack-up)
Average expected depth	1981 m

RESERVES	
Crude oil	21×10^6 tonnes

BEATRICE DRILLING PLATFORM

GENERAL	
Name	Beatrice Drilling Platform
Installation date	September 1979
Fabricating company	Dragados y Construcciones
Fabrication site	Almeria, Spain
Type of jacket	Steel, twin platform adjacent to production platform
Number of legs	8
Standard well conductors	32
Subsea well conductors	0
Production capacity	80,000 bbl/day
Storage capacity	0

SUBSTRUCTURE	
Piles driven	18
Total weight steel for piles	4500 tonnes
Weight structural steel for jacket and deck	4600 tonnes
Total weight jacket and deck (excluding modules and equipment)	4600 tonnes

SUPERSTRUCTURE	
Type of deck	Steel, cellar with two parts that stab into supporting legs
Weight of modules and equipment	3538 tonnes

BEATRICE PRODUCTION PLATFORM

GENERAL	
Name	Beatrice Production Platform
Installation date	May 1980
Fabricating company	Dragados y Construcciones/Brown and Root
Fabrication site	Almeria, Spain (jacket); Ardersier, Scotland (deck, modules)
Type of jacket	Steel, adjacent to drilling platform
Number of legs	8
Standard well conductors	0 (twin production platform adjacent to drilling platform)
Subsea well conductors	0
Production capacity	0 (80,000 bbl/day from twin drilling platform)
Storage capacity	0

SUBSTRUCTURE	
Piles driven	18
Total weight steel for piles	4500 tonnes
Weight structural steel for jacket and deck	4300 tonnes
Total weight jacket and deck (excluding modules and equipment)	4300 tonnes

SUPERSTRUCTURE	
Type of deck	Steel
Weight of modules and equipment	4973 tonnes

ZAPATA NORDIC PLATFORM

GENERAL	
Name	Zapata Nordic
Installation date	Contracted March 1979
Owner company	Zapata Offshore
Type of jacket	Converted jack-up
Number of legs	3 (jack-up)
Standard well conductors	12
Subsea well conductors	0
Production capacity	16,000 bbl/day
Storage capacity	0

SUBSTRUCTURE	
Total weight jack-up platform (including modules and equipment)	8200 tonnes
Weight steel for drilling conductor	440 tonnes (jacket), 174 tonnes (deck)

BEATRICE ANCILLARY FACILITIES

FIELD-TO-SHORE PIPELINES		
Function	Outside diameter (in.)	Length (km)
Oil: Beatrice—Old Sandwick, Shetlands	16	72

FIGURE 7.4 The converted jack-up rig *Zapata Nordic*, employed in the north-east section of Beatrice field. (By courtesy of BNOC.)

BERYL A

The Beryl A field was discovered in September 1972 and is being developed by Mobil. Reserves are estimated as 66 million tonnes, and oil is currently being produced from wells drilled from a single concrete platform. Production began in 1976 and it is expected that the peak production rate of 5 million tonnes/year will be achieved in 1980. Nine new development wells were started during 1979, and pressure in the upper Beryl reservoir is being maintained by gas and water injection. The oil is transported to shore using tankers which are loaded at a Single Point Mooring (SPM) facility.

It is expected that Mobil will also develop the Beryl B structure, located in the northern portion of Block 9/13; an additional fixed steel platform would be required, with the new production being piped to the Beryl A platform. If Beryl B is developed, this would raise the reserves of the entire Beryl field to an estimated 107 million tonnes (800 million barrels).

BERYL A FIELD

GENERAL	
Name	Beryl A
Location	Block 9/13a
Operator	Mobil Producing North Sea Ltd.
Company interest	Mobil Producing North Sea Ltd. (50%); Amerada Exploration Ltd. (20%); Texas Eastern (UK) Ltd. (20%); BGC (10%)
Discovery date	September 1972
Production date	June 1976
Peak production rate	5×10^6 tonnes/year in 1980
API gravity of crude oil	$39.6°$
Number of platforms	1 (Beryl A)
ENVIRONMENT	
Water depth	117 m
Geological structure	Permo-Triassic (undifferentiated)
Dimension of geological structure	210 km^2
DISCOVERY DRILLING	
Dry wells before discovery well	0
Appraisal wells after discovery well	3
Total wells to determine viability	4 (including discovery well)
PRODUCTION DRILLING	
Total wells anticipated (including reinjection wells)	41
Average expected depth	3810 m
RESERVES	
Crude oil	66×10^6 tonnes

BERYL A PLATFORM

GENERAL	
Name	Beryl A
Installation date	July 1975
Fabricating company	Condeep Group
Fabrication site	Stavanger, Norway
Building time (contract to installation)	21 months
Type of jacket	Concrete
Number of legs	3
Vertical height (from mud line to lowest deck)	143.2 m
Standard well conductors	40
Subsea well conductors	4
Production capacity	4×10^6 tonnes/year
Storage capacity	900,000 bbl

SUBSTRUCTURE	
Weight structural steel for jacket	630 tonnes (skirt)
Weight reinforcing steel for jacket	9000 tonnes
Weight prestressed steel for jacket	3000 tonnes
Total weight concrete for jacket	192,000 tonnes
Total volume concrete for jacket	59,462 m^3
Total weight jacket (excluding deck, modules and equipment)	204,630 tonnes

SUPERSTRUCTURE	
Type of deck	Steel, plate
Weight of deck	6962 tonnes
Weight of modules and equipment	20,000 tonnes

BERYL A ANCILLARY FACILITIES

OFFSHORE INTRA-FIELD PIPELINES		
Function	*Outside diameter (in.)*	*Length (km)*
Oil: Beryl A platform—"SM" (see below)	32	1.74

FIELD TERMINAL LOADING SYSTEM	
Terminal construction	Single-Point Mooring (SPM)
Storage capacity	0
Total weight	1400 tonnes

TANKERS	
Number	2 (Matco Avon (formerly Mobil Valiant), Matco Thames)
Weight	80,000 tonnes deadweight each

REMOTE VENT/FLARE	
Flare construction	Steel flare bridge from platform to steel and concrete truss tower
Weight of steel	1050 tonnes (flare bridge)
Weight of concrete	1200 tonnes (tower); 15,000 tonnes (tower support base)
Total weight	17,250 tonnes

FIGURE 7.5 Beryl A platform. (By courtesy of Mobil Producing North Sea Ltd.)

BRAE

The Brae field was discovered in April 1975, and the southern portion of the field, which is estimated to have recoverable reserves of 36 million tonnes, will be developed by Marathon Oil using a single platform. Production is expected to begin in 1983 and the crude oil and natural-gas liquids will be transported to shore via a spur line into BP's Forties—Cruden Bay pipeline. Gas will be reinjected until a gas-gathering line is completed.

There is also potential for the future development of the central and northern parts of the Brae structure. Additional drilling is planned during 1980 to evaluate the reserves of these areas.

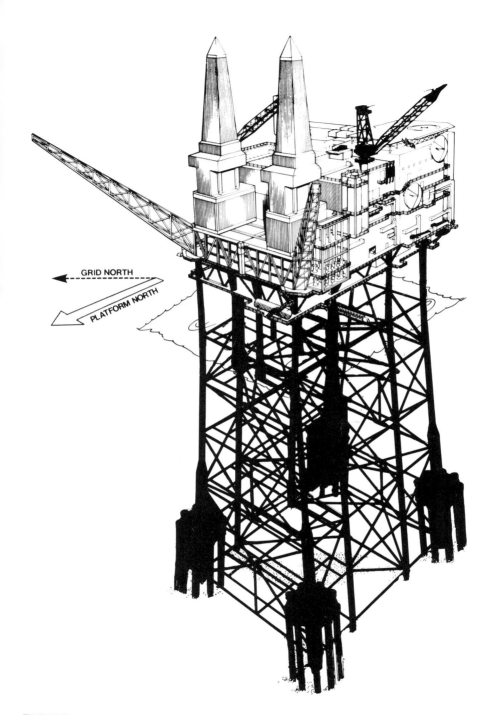

FIGURE 7.6 Artist's impression of Brae A platform. (By courtesy of Marathon Oil Co.)

BRAE FIELD

GENERAL	
Name	Brae
Location	Block 16/7a
Operator	Marathon Oil Co.
Company interest	Marathon Oil North Sea (GB) Ltd. (38%); BNOC (20%); Bow Valley Exploration (UK) Ltd. (14%); Sunningdale Oil (UK) Ltd. (8%); Kaiser Exploration (UK) Ltd. (6.3%); LL and E (UK) Inc. (6.3%); Siebens Oil and Gas (UK) Ltd. (4%); Saga Petroleum (UK) Ltd. (2%); Kaiser Canadian Oil (UK) Ltd.(1.4%)
Discovery date	April 1975
Production date	Expected 1983
Peak production rate	4.9×10^6 tonnes/year
API gravity of crude oil	$35°$
Number of platforms	1 (Brae)

ENVIRONMENT	
Water depth	103 m
Geological structure	Upper Jurassic
Dimension of geological structure	Not yet totally defined as appraisal well drilling continues in northern part of field

DISCOVERY DRILLING	
Total wells to determine viability	18 (14 in block, 4 delineation wells)

PRODUCTION DRILLING	
Total wells anticipated	36 (19 production, 14 water injection, 3 gas injection)
Average expected depth	3800 m

BRAE FIELD (continued)

RESERVES	
Crude oil	36×10^6 tonnes (southern Brae only)
Gas	1.3×10^{12} scf

BRAE PLATFORM

GENERAL	
Name	Brae
Installation date	Expected April 1982
Platform design contractor	Brown and Root
Fabricating company	McDermott
Fabrication site	Ardersier, Scotland
Building time (contract to installation)	$\sim$ 24 months
Type of jacket	Steel
Number of legs	8
Standard well conductors	46
Subsea well conductors	0
Production capacity	100,000 bbl/day (oil); 12,000 bbl/day (natural-gas liquids)
Storage capacity	0
SUBSTRUCTURE	
Piles driven	32
Total weight steel for piles	11,600 tonnes
Weight structural steel for jacket and deck	16,000 tonnes
Total weight jacket (including deck, but excluding modules and equipment)	16,000 tonnes

BRAE PLATFORM (continued)

SUPERSTRUCTURE	
Type of deck	Skid, acts as part of jacket-form support for modules
Weight of modules and equipment	31,000 tonnes

BRAE ANCILLARY FACILITIES

OFFSHORE INTER-FIELD PIPELINES		
Function	*Outside diameter (in.)*	*Length (km)*
Oil: Brae—Forties	24	113

BRENT

The Brent field was discovered in July 1971, and it remains one of the largest North Sea oil fields, with estimated recoverable reserves of 229 million tonnes and an expected peak production rate of 23 million tonnes/year (173 million barrels/year) in 1984. The operating company is Shell. Four platforms have been needed to develop the field, three concrete and one steel; a total of 136 development wells are anticipated over the life of the field. A complex system of intra-field pipelines connects platforms A, B, and D with the central platform C which is to act as the main export pumping station. The pipeline network also allows all platforms to be connected to the remote flare vent and the tanker loading facility (SPAR). During 1979 the SPAR facility was the only means of transporting oil away from the field, and the average production rate of over 200,000 barrels/day placed heavy demands on the system; due to problems with industrial relations Brent C platform was not tied into the export pipeline to Sullom Voe until November 1979.

FIGURE 7.7 Gas being flared from a safety vent in the Brent field. (By courtesy of Shell U.K. Ltd.)

BRENT FIELD

GENERAL	
Name	Brent
Location	Block 211/29
Operator	Shell (UK) Ltd.
Company interest	Shell (50%); Esso (50%)
Discovery date	July 1971
Production date	November 1976
Peak production rate	23×10^6 tonnes/year
API gravity of crude oil	$35°$
Number of platforms	4 (Brent A,B,C,D)

ENVIRONMENT	
Water depth	140 m
Geological structure	Jurassic/Magnus/Brent
Dimension of geological structure	16.1 km^2

DISCOVERY DRILLING	
Dry wells before discovery well	1
Appraisal wells after discovery well	5
Total wells to determine viability	7 (including discovery well)

PRODUCTION DRILLING	
Total wells anticipated (including reinjection wells)	136
Average expected depth	2996–4267 m

RESERVES	
Crude oil	229×10^6 tonnes
Gas	2×10^{12} scf

BRENT A PLATFORM

GENERAL	
Name	Brent A
Installation date	May 1976
Fabricating company	Redpath, Dorman and Long (North Sea) Ltd.
Fabrication site	Methil, Scotland
Building time (contract to installation)	42 months
Type of jacket	Steel
Number of legs	6
Vertical height (from mud line to lowest deck)	150.8 m
Standard well conductors	28
Subsea well conductors	0
Production capacity	100,000 bbl/day (oil); 2×10^8 scf/day (gas)
Storage capacity	0
SUBSTRUCTURE	
Piles driven	32
Average depth driven	30.48 m
Total weight steel for piles	7200 tonnes
Weight structural steel for jacket	14,000 tonnes
Total weight jacket (excluding deck, modules, and equipment)	14,000 tonnes
SUPERSTRUCTURE	
Type of deck	Steel, plate and girder
Weight of deck	1800 tonnes
Weight of modules and equipment	9580 tonnes

132

FIGURE 7.8 Brent A platform. (By courtesy of Shell U.K. Ltd.)

BRENT B PLATFORM

GENERAL	
Name	Brent B
Installation date	August 1975
Fabricating company	Condeep Group
Fabrication site	Stavanger, Norway
Building time (contract to installation)	24 months
Type of jacket	Concrete with steel skirt
Number of legs	3
Vertical height	207.2 m (mud line—lowest deck)
Standard well conductors	38
Subsea well conductors	0
Production capacity	160,000 bbl/day (oil); 320×10^6 scf/day (gas)
Storage capacity	1,100,000 bbl

SUBSTRUCTURE	
Weight structural steel for jacket	900 tonnes
Weight reinforcing steel for jacket	10,000 tonnes
Weight prestressed steel for jacket	1600 tonnes
Total weight concrete for jacket	153,770 tonnes
Total volume concrete for jacket	70,000 m^3
Total weight jacket (excluding deck, modules, and equipment)	166,270 tonnes

SUPERSTRUCTURE	
Type of deck	Steel, plate and girder
Weight of deck	3100 tonnes
Weight of modules and equipment	11,590 tonnes

FIGURE 7.9 Brent B platform. (By courtesy of Shell U.K. Ltd.)

BRENT C PLATFORM

GENERAL	
Name	Brent C
Installation date	June 1978
Fabricating company	McAlpine/Sea Tank
Fabrication site	Ardyne Point, Scotland
Building time (contract to installation)	60 months
Type of jacket	Concrete
Number of legs	4
Vertical height (from mud line to lowest deck)	164.5 m
Standard well conductors	40
Subsea well conductors	0
Production capacity	150,000 bbl/day (oil); 350×10^6 scf/day (gas)
Storage capacity	550,000 bbl

SUBSTRUCTURE	
Weight reinforcing steel for jacket	14,000 tonnes
Weight prestressed steel for jacket	1100 tonnes
Total weight concrete for jacket	267,900 tonnes
Total volume concrete for jacket	107,500 m^3
Total weight jacket (excluding deck, modules, and equipment)	283,000 tonnes

SUPERSTRUCTURE	
Type of deck	Steel, girder lattice
Weight of deck	6400 tonnes
Weight of modules and equipment	13,280 tonnes

136

FIGURE 7.10 The substructure of Brent C platform being towed out from Ardyne Point on the west coast of Scotland. (By courtesy of Shell U.K. Ltd.)

BRENT D PLATFORM

GENERAL	
Name	Brent D
Installation date	July 1976
Fabricating company	Condeep Group
Fabrication site	Stavanger, Norway
Building time (contract to installation)	26 months
Type of jacket	Concrete with steel skirt
Number of legs	3
Vertical height	167.2 m (mud line—lowest deck)
Standard well conductors	48
Subsea well conductors	0
Production capacity	150,000 bbl/day (oil); 350×10^6 scf/day (gas)
Storage capacity	1,100,000 bbl

SUBSTRUCTURE	
Weight structural steel for jacket	630 tonnes (estimate based on Beryl A)
Weight reinforcing steel for jacket	14,000 tonnes
Weight prestressed steel for jacket	1400 tonnes
Total weight concrete for jacket	158,970 tonnes
Total volume concrete for jacket	75,000 m^3
Total weight jacket (excluding deck, modules, and equipment)	175,000 tonnes

SUPERSTRUCTURE	
Type of deck	Steel, plate and girder
Weight of deck	3200 tonnes
Weight of modules and equipment	11,200 tonnes

FIGURE 7.11 Brent D platform. (By courtesy of Shell U.K. Ltd.)

BRENT ANCILLARY FACILITIES

OFFSHORE INTRA-FIELD PIPELINES		
Function	*Outside diameter (in.)*	*Length (km)*
Oil: Brent B —"SPAR" (see below)	16	3.5
Brent A—"SPAR" (see below)	16	3.0
Brent C—Brent B	24	4.4
Brent D—Brent C	20	4.2
Gas: Brent B—Brent A	36	2.4
Brent A—flare	28	4.0
Brent B—flare	36	3.0
Brent C—Brent B	30	4.4
Brent D—Brent C	24	4.2

OFFSHORE INTER-FIELD PIPELINES		
Function	*Outside diameter (in.)*	*Length (km)*
Oil: Brent C—South Cormorant	30	36.0

FIELD-TO-SHORE PIPELINES		
Function	*Outside diameter (in.)*	*Length (km)*
Oil: South Cormorant—Sullom Voe, Shetlands (shared line carrying oil from South Cormorant, Brent, Dunlin, Murchison, and Thistle fields)	36	150
Gas: Brent A—St. Fergus, Scotland	36	450

FIGURE 7.12 Free-floating storage and tanker loading facility (SPAR) in the Brent field. (By courtesy of Shell U.K. Ltd.)

141

BRENT ANCILLARY FACILITIES (continued)

FIELD TERMINAL LOADING SYSTEM	
Terminal construction	Free-floating spar storage and loading facility (SPAR)
Storage capacity	300,000 bbl
Overall height	141.1 m
Weight of steel	59,200 tonnes
Weight of ballast	6800 tonnes
Total weight	66,000 tonnes (excluding anchor and chain)
Weight of anchor	7200 tonnes
Cargo pumps	4 (700 h.p. each)
Power supply	4 gas-turbine-driven generators running on diesel fuel

TANKERS	
Number	4 (Aberdeen, Warwickshire, Drupa, Serenia)
Weight	Aberdeen, 90,000 tonnes deadweight; Warwickshire, 85,000 tonnes deadweight; Drupa, 70,871 tonnes deadweight; Serenia, 65,000 tonnes deadweight

REMOTE VENT/FLARE	
Flare construction	Welded lattice structure of triangular cross-section fabricated from steel tube
Overall height	197.5 m
Total weight	1250 tonnes

BUCHAN

Buchan was discovered in August 1974 and the field is being developed by British Petroleum. With estimated recoverable reserves of 6.8 million tonnes, Buchan is one of the smaller oil fields in the U.K. sector. The semi-submersible *Drillmaster* rig has been converted to serve as a floating production platform, and a peak production rate of 7.2 million tonnes/year is anticipated. Production from the field is expected to begin in August 1980, which is about one year later than originally planned; most of the delay has been caused by the complexity of the conversion work on the *Drillmaster* rig. Oil from the field will be transported to shore by two 100,000-tonne tankers loaded from a Catenary Anchor Leg Mooring (CALM) facility.

BUCHAN FIELD

GENERAL

Name	Buchan
Location	Block 21/1a
Operator	British Petroleum Ltd. (BP)
Company interest	BP Dev. Ltd. (27.08%); Can Del Petroleum (UK) Ltd. (14%); City Petroleum Co. (14%); St. Joe Petroleum (UK) Ltd. (14%); Transworld Petroleum (UK) Ltd. (14%); CCP North Sea Ass. Ltd. (6.35%); Gas and Oil Acreage Ltd. (5%); Charterhall Oil North Sea Ltd. (4.23%); Lochiel Exploration (1%); Charterhall Oil Ltd. (0.33%)
Discovery date	August 1974
Production date	Expected 1980
Peak production rate	2.2×10^6 tonnes/year
API gravity of crude oil	$33.5°$
Number of platforms	1 (Buchan)

ENVIRONMENT

Water depth	120 m
Geological structure	Over-pressured highly fractured sandstone

DISCOVERY DRILLING

Total wells to determine viability	5

PRODUCTION DRILLING

Total wells anticipated (including reinjection wells)	7 (4 through template; 3 satellite wells); a fourth satellite well may be drilled in 1980
Average expected depth	3200 m

RESERVES

Crude oil	6.8×10^6 tonnes

144

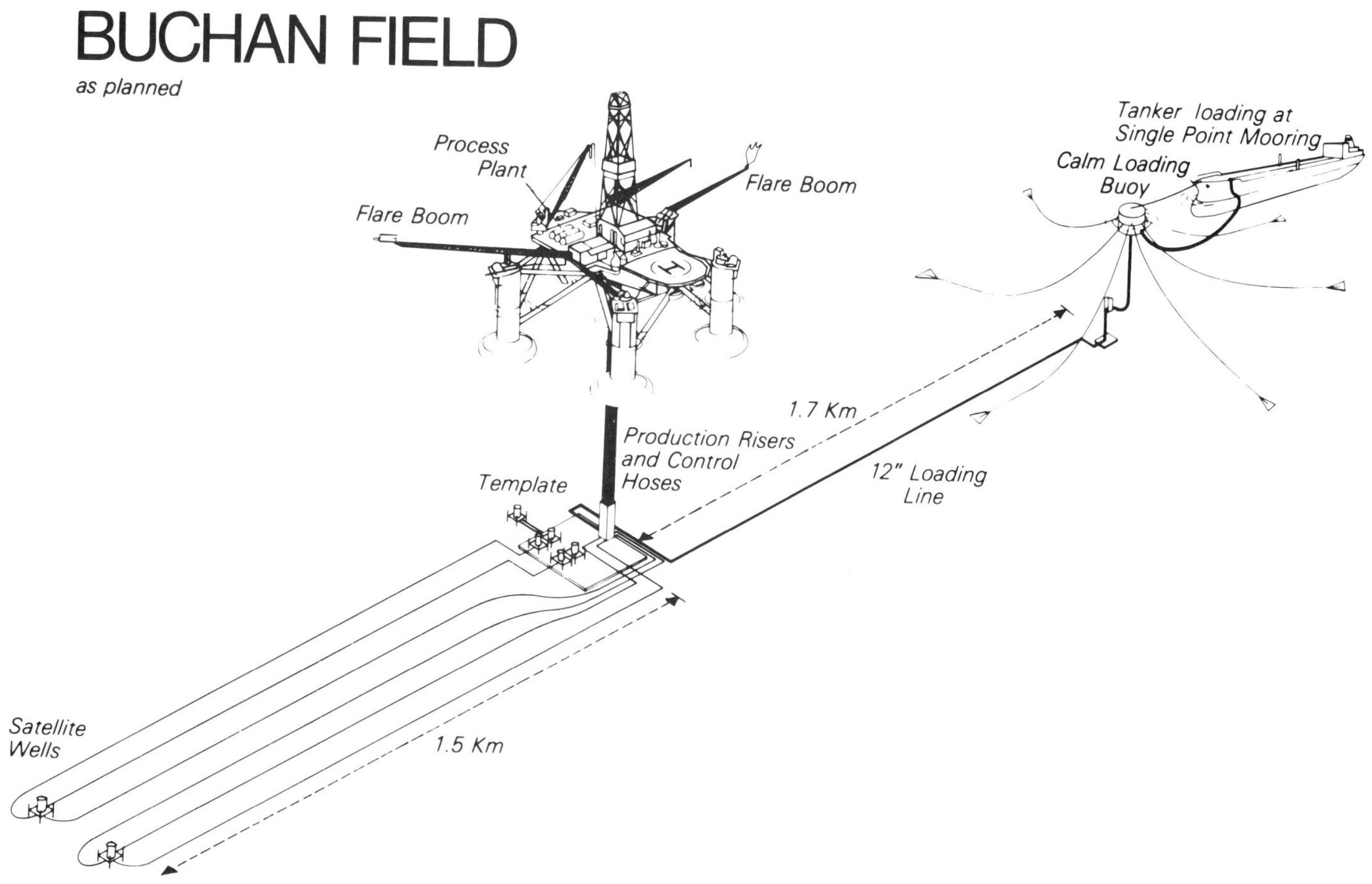

BUCHAN FIELD
as planned

Tanker loading at
Single Point Mooring

Calm Loading
Buoy

Flare Boom

Process
Plant

Flare Boom

12" Loading
Line

1.7 Km

Production Risers
and Control
Hoses

Template

1.5 Km

Satellite
Wells

FIGURE 7.13 Schematic diagram of the production and tanker-loading facilities in Buchan field. (By courtesy of British Petroleum.)

BUCHAN PLATFORM

GENERAL	
Name	Buchan
Installation date	May 1980
Modification company	Lewis Offshore
Modification site	Stornoway, Lewis, Scotland
Type of jacket	Steel, semi-submersible "Drillmaster"
Number of legs	4
Standard well conductors	8-slot capacity seabed drilling template
Subsea well conductors	3 (1 is 6 m from template; 2 are 1.5 km from riser)
Riser capacity	19 (8 pairs for production; 2 service lines for flushing; 1 export line of 12-in. diameter)
Production capacity	75,000 bbl/day
Storage capacity	12,000 bbl
SUBSTRUCTURE	
Weight steel for drilling conductor	83 tonnes
Weight structural steel for jacket	18,083 tonnes
Total weight jacket (excluding deck, modules, and equipment)	18,083 tonnes
SUPERSTRUCTURE	
Weight of deck, modules, and equipment	3000 tonnes

146

FIGURE 7.14 Conversion work in progress on the semi-submersible *Drillmaster* rig, destined to be the production platform in Buchan field: a night view in Glumaig Harbour, Stornoway. (By courtesy of British Petroleum.)

BUCHAN ANCILLARY FACILITIES

OFFSHORE INTRA-FIELD PIPELINES		
Function	*Outside diameter (in.)*	*Length (km)*
Oil: riser—"CALM" (see below)	12	1.7
riser—satellite wells	4	1.5 total (4 lines)

FIELD TERMINAL LOADING SYSTEM	
Terminal construction	Press-Imodo, Catenary Anchor Leg Mooring (CALM) system tanker loading buoy
Overall dimensions	15.2 m (diameter) $\times$ 4.57 m (depth)
Mooring system	Buoy moored by 6 anchor legs, each $\sim$ 407 m long
Total weight	270 tonnes (at load out); 500 tonnes (displacement)

TANKERS	
Number	2; to be used for loading from "CALM" (see above)
Weight	100,000 tonnes deadweight each

CLAYMORE

Claymore field was discovered in May 1974 and is being developed by Occidental Petroleum. By North Sea standards the field is moderately large, with estimated recoverable reserves of 55 million tonnes. Twenty-four of the thirty-six wells anticipated are being drilled from a single fixed steel platform. Production began in November 1977, and a peak production rate of 4.5 million tonnes/year is expected in 1980. Oil is transported from the field via pipeline to the Piper system and subsequently to Flotta.

CLAYMORE FIELD

GENERAL	
Name	Claymore
Location	Block 14/19
Operator	Occidental Petroleum (UK) Ltd.
Company interest	Occidental Petroleum (Caledonia) Ltd. (36.5%); Getty Oil International (Britain) Ltd. (23.5%); Allied Chemical (GB) Ltd. (20%); Thomson North Sea Ltd. (20%)
Discovery date	May 1974
Production date	November 1977
Peak production rate	4.5×10^6 tonnes/year
API gravity of crude oil	$30°$
Number of platforms	1 (Claymore A)
ENVIRONMENT	
Water depth	109.7 m
Geological structure	Middle Jurassic
Dimension of geological structure	Circular, diameter ~8.4 km
DISCOVERY DRILLING	
Dry wells before discovery well	1
Appraisal wells after discovery well	6
Total wells to determine viability (including discovery well)	8 (excluding 1 well redrilled but including 4 drilled on edge of field)
PRODUCTION DRILLING	
Total wells anticipated	36 (including reinjection wells)
Average expected depth	3658 m
RESERVES	
Crude oil	55×10^6 tonnes

CLAYMORE A PLATFORM

GENERAL	
Name	Claymore A
Installation date	July 1976
Fabricating company	Union Industrielle et d'Enterprise
Fabrication site	Cherbourg, France
Building time (contract to installation)	30 months
Type of jacket	Steel
Number of legs	4
Standard well conductors	36
Subsea well conductors	0
Production capacity	168,000 bbl/day
Storage capacity	0

SUBSTRUCTURE	
Piles driven	24
Average depth driven	38.5 m
Total weight steel for piles	3135 tonnes
Weight structural steel for jacket	9286 tonnes
Total weight jacket (excluding deck, modules, and equipment)	9286 tonnes (including pile steeves, pile guides, and launch runner)

SUPERSTRUCTURE	
Type of deck	Steel
Weight of deck	1000 tonnes
Weight of modules and equipment	12,286 tonnes

FIGURE 7.15 Claymore A platform. (By courtesy of Occidental Petroleum.)

CLAYMORE ANCILLARY FACILITIES

OFFSHORE INTER-FIELD PIPELINES		
Function	*Outside diameter (in.)*	*Length (km)*
Oil: Claymore A–Piper pipeline (30 in.)	30	14.48

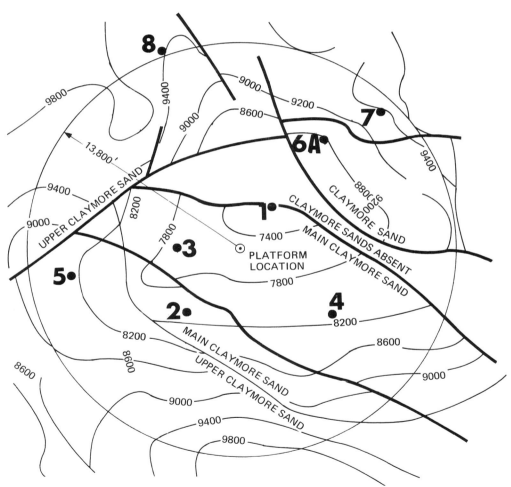

FIGURE 7.16 Geological strata in Claymore field.

DUNLIN

Dunlin was discovered in July 1973 and came into production in August 1978. It is a medium-sized field, with recoverable reserves estimated at 41 million tonnes; a peak production rate of 5.9 million tonnes/year is expected in 1980. The operating company, Shell, is employing a single concrete platform to develop the field. During 1979 three new wells were completed, making a total of five production and three water-injection wells in operation by the end of 1979. Production rates from Dunlin have been higher than originally expected.

FIGURE 7.17 Dunlin A platform. (By courtesy of Shell Oil.)

DUNLIN FIELD

GENERAL	
Name	Dunlin
Location	Blocks 211/23a and 211/24a
Operator	Shell (UK) Ltd.
Company interest	Shell (50%); Esso (50%)
Discovery date	July 1973
Production date	August 1978
Peak production rate	5.9×10^6 tonnes/year in 1980
API gravity of crude oil	$34.9°$
Number of platforms	1 (Dunlin A)

ENVIRONMENT	
Water depth	151 m
Geological structure	Upper and Middle Jurassic
Dimension of geological structure	60 km^2

DISCOVERY DRILLING	
Dry wells before discovery well	1
Appraisal wells after discovery well (including any dry wells)	5
Total wells to determine viability (including discovery well)	7

PRODUCTION DRILLING	
Total wells anticipated (including reinjection wells)	45
Average expected depth	3048 m

RESERVES	
Crude oil	41×10^6 tonnes

DUNLIN A PLATFORM

GENERAL	
Name	Dunlin A
Installation date	May 1977
Fabricating company	Andoc
Fabrication site	Rotterdam, Netherlands;Stord, Norway
Building time (contract to installation)	36 months
Type of jacket	Concrete
Number of legs	4
Vertical height	173.9 m (mud line—lowest deck)
Standard well conductors	48
Subsea well conductors	0
Production capacity	150,000 bbl/day (oil); 40×10^6 scf/day (gas)
Storage capacity	800,000 bbl

SUBSTRUCTURE	
Weight structural steel for jacket	1450 tonnes (1000 piping, 450 columns)
Weight reinforcing steel for jacket	9500 tonnes
Weight prestressed steel for jacket	3000 tonnes
Total weight concrete for jacket	211,050 tonnes
Total volume concrete for jacket	90,000 m^3
Total weight jacket (excluding deck, modules, and equipment)	225,000

SUPERSTRUCTURE	
Type of deck	Steel, box girder
Weight of deck	3800 tonnes
Weight of modules and equipment	11,300 tonnes

DUNLIN ANCILLARY FACILITIES

OFFSHORE INTER-FIELD PIPELINES		
Function	*Outside diameter (in.)*	*Length (km)*
Oil: Dunlin—South Cormorant	24	31.5

FORTIES

British Petroleum's Forties field, discovered in November 1970, is the U.K. sector's largest producer of oil. Output from the field ranges from 500,000 to 550,000 barrels/day, and in 1979 facilities for the recovery of natural-gas liquids were installed on each of the production platforms, increasing the total expected production rate by 25,000 barrels/day. The recoverable reserves of the Forties field are estimated to be 240 million tonnes, making it the largest field yet discovered in the U.K. sector. The four steel production platforms were installed in 1974/1975. Oil is transported by pipeline to the shore at Cruden Bay, and from there to the Grangemouth refining facilities.

FORTIES FIELD

GENERAL	
Name	Forties
Location	Blocks 21/10 and 22/6a
Operator	BP Oil Development Ltd.
Company interest	BP Oil Development Ltd. (100%)
Discovery date	November 1970
Production date	November 1975
Peak production rate	24×10^6 tonnes/year in 1978
API gravity of crude oil	$37°$
Number of platforms	4 (FA, FB, FC, FD)

ENVIRONMENT	
Water depth	103.6—128.0 m
Geological structure	Tertiary
Dimension of geological structure	16.09×12.95 km^2

DISCOVERY DRILLING	
Dry wells before discovery well	0
Appraisal wells after discovery well (including any dry wells)	4
Total wells to determine viability (including discovery well)	5

PRODUCTION DRILLING	
Total wells anticipated (including reinjection wells)	106
Average expected depth	2450—3500 m

RESERVES	
Crude oil	240×10^6 tonnes

FA PLATFORM (GRAYTHORP I)

GENERAL	
Name	FA(Graythorp I)
Installation date	July 1974
Fabricating company	Laing Offshore
Fabrication site	Teesside, England
Building time (contract to installation)	29 months
Type of jacket	Steel
Number of legs	4
Vertical height (from mud line to lowest deck)	129.5 m
Standard well conductors	27
Subsea well conductors	0
Production capacity	125,000 bbl/day
Storage capacity	0

SUBSTRUCTURE	
Piles driven	36
Depth driven	67.1–76.2 m
Total weight steel for piles	6428.3 tonnes
Total weight grout for pile setting	541 tonnes
Weight structural steel for jacket	15,436 tonnes (including well conductors and pile guides)
Total weight jacket (excluding deck, modules, and equipment)	15,436 tonnes

SUPERSTRUCTURE	
Type of deck	Steel, integral part of modules
Weight of modules and equipment	10,551 tonnes

FB PLATFORM (GRAYTHORP II)

GENERAL	
Name	FB (Graythorp II)
Installation date	June 1975
Fabricating company	Laing Offshore
Fabrication site	Teesside, England
Type of jacket	Steel
Number of legs	4
Vertical height (from mud line to lowest deck)	150.3 m
Standard well conductors	26
Subsea well conductors	0
Production capacity	125,000 bbl/day
Storage capacity	0

SUBSTRUCTURE	
Piles driven	44
Depth driven	67.1–76.2 m
Total weight steel for piles	7417 tonnes
Total weight grout for pile setting	661 tonnes
Weight structural steel for jacket	18,253 tonnes (including well conductors and pile guides)
Total weight jacket (excluding deck, modules, and equipment)	18,253 tonnes

SUPERSTRUCTURE	
Type of deck	Steel, integral part of modules
Weight of modules and equipment	10,551 tonnes

FIGURE 7.18 Forties FB platform (Graythorp II). (By courtesy of British Petroleum.)

FC PLATFORM (HIGHLANDS ONE)

GENERAL	
Name	FC (Highlands One)
Installation date	August 1974
Fabricating company	Highlands Fabricators
Fabrication site	Nigg Bay, Scotland
Building time (contract to installation)	31 months
Type of jacket	Steel
Number of legs	4
Vertical height (from mud line to lowest deck)	141.1 m
Standard well conductors	27
Subsea well conductors	0
Production capacity	125,000 bbl/day
Storage capacity	0

SUBSTRUCTURE	
Piles driven	44
Depth driven	60.9–73.1 m
Total weight steel for piles	7417 tonnes
Total weight grout for pile setting	661 tonnes
Weight structural steel for jacket	18,398 tonnes (including well conductors and pile guides)
Total weight jacket (excluding deck, modules, and equipment)	18,398 tonnes

SUPERSTRUCTURE	
Type of deck	Steel, integral part of modules
Weight of modules and equipment	10,551 tonnes

164

FIGURE 7.19 Forties FC platform (Highlands One). (By courtesy of British Petroleum.)

FD PLATFORM (HIGHLANDS TWO)

GENERAL	
Name	FD (Highlands Two)
Installation date	June 1975
Fabricating company	Highlands Fabricators
Fabrication site	Nigg Bay, Scotland
Type of jacket	Steel
Number of legs	4
Vertical height (from mud line to lowest deck)	141.1 m
Standard well conductors	26
Subsea well conductors	0
Production capacity	125,000 bbl/day
Storage capacity	0

SUBSTRUCTURE	
Piles driven	44
Depth driven	60.9–73.1 m
Total weight steel for piles	7417 tonnes
Total weight grout for pile setting	661 tonnes
Weight structural steel for jacket	16,892 tonnes (including well conductors and pile guides)
Total weight jacket (excluding deck, modules, and equipment)	16,892 tonnes

SUPERSTRUCTURE	
Type of deck	Steel, integral part of modules
Weight of modules and equipment	10,551 tonnes

166

FIGURE 7.20 Forties FD platform (Highlands Two). (By courtesy of British Petroleum.)

FORTIES ANCILLARY FACILITIES

OFFSHORE INTRA-FIELD PIPELINES		
Function	*Outside diameter (in.)*	*Length (km)*
Oil: FB—FC	20	5
FA—FC	20	7.75
FD—FC	20	3.6
FIELD-TO-SHORE PIPELINES		
Function	*Outside diameter (in.)*	*Length (km)*
Oil: FC—Cruden Bay, Scotland	32	176

FULMAR

The Fulmar field was discovered in November 1975 and is one of the larger fields currently under development, with estimated reserves of 70 million tonnes. The field is being developed by Shell/Esso who have installed a main steel platform and a satellite well-head jacket. It is anticipated that a total of twenty-eight wells will be needed; production is scheduled to begin in 1981 and the field is expected to have an eventual peak production rate of 180,000 barrels/day (equivalent to 8.6 million tonnes/year). Oil produced from the field will be loaded into the permanently moored tanker *Medora* using a Single Anchor Leg Mooring (SALM) system. The *Medora* will provide buffer storage equivalent to eight days' peak production, and will simultaneously offload oil into other tankers for transport to the shore. The proposed SALM loading facility will be the largest of its kind in the world.

FULMAR FIELD

GENERAL	
Name	Fulmar
Location	Block 30/16
Operator	Shell/Esso
Company interest	Shell (42.5%); Esso (42.5%); Amoco (3.87%); BGC (3.87%); Mobil (3.0%); Amerada (2.71%); North Sea (1.55%)
Discovery date	November 1975
Production date	Expected 1981
Peak production rate	8.6×10^6 tonnes/year
API gravity of crude oil	$40°$
Number of platforms	2 (Fulmar A, B)

ENVIRONMENT	
Water depth	82 m
Geological structure	Upper Jurassic
Dimension of geological structure	Approximately circular, diameter 4 km

DISCOVERY DRILLING	
Total wells to determine viability	2

PRODUCTION DRILLING	
Total wells anticipated	28 (16 production, of which 4 on well-head jacket; 10 water injection; 2 gas injection)
Average expected depth	3048–3292 m

RESERVES	
Crude oil	70×10^6 tonnes
Gas	190×10^9 scf

FULMAR MAIN JACKET (A)

GENERAL	
Name	Fulmar Main Jacket (A)
Installation date	June 1980
Fabricating company	Highland Fabricators
Fabrication site	Nigg Bay, Scotland
Building time (contract to installation)	24 months
Type of jacket	Steel
Number of legs	8
Standard well conductors	36
Subsea well conductors	0
Production capacity	180,000 bbl/day
Storage capacity	1.5×10^6 bbl, using permanently moored tanker

SUBSTRUCTURE	
Piles driven	32
Total weight steel for piles	5000 tonnes
Weight structural steel for jacket	12,500 tonnes
Total weight jacket (excluding deck, modules, and equipment)	12,500 tonnes

SUPERSTRUCTURE	
Type of deck	Steel
Weight of deck	4900 tonnes
Weight of modules and equipment	22,500 tonnes

FULMAR WELL-HEAD PLATFORM (B)

GENERAL	
Name	Fulmar Well-head Platform (B)
Installation date	1979
Fabricating company	Redpath de Groot Caledonian
Fabrication site	Methil, Scotland
Type of jacket	Steel; 54.9 m from main production jacket A, connected by bridge
Number of legs	4
Standard well conductors	Expected 6 (4 drilled by June 1980, a fifth anticipated)
Subsea well conductors	0
Production capacity	0 (linked by bridge to production jacket A)
Storage capacity	0

SUBSTRUCTURE	
Piles driven	8
Total weight steel for piles	~ 1000 tonnes
Weight structural steel for jacket	1570 tonnes
Total weight jacket (excluding deck)	1570 tonnes

SUPERSTRUCTURE	
Type of deck	Steel
Weight of deck	250 tonnes

FIGURE 7.21 The substructure and deck of Fulmar well-head platform (B). (By courtesy of Shell Oil.)

FULMAR ANCILLARY FACILITIES

OFFSHORE INTRA-FIELD PIPELINES		
Function	*Outside diameter (in.)*	*Length (km)*
Oil: Fulmar A—"SALM" (see below)	16	2.4

FIELD TERMINAL LOADING SYSTEM	
Terminal construction	Single Anchor Leg Mooring (SALM)
Storage capacity	0 (permanently moored tanker used)
Overall dimensions	83 m (height), 16 m (maximum diameter)
Weight of arm assembly	900 tonnes
Weight of buoy	6900 tonnes (gross buoyancy); 2100 tonnes (gross weight); 2600 tonnes (ballast)
Weight of U-joint	360 tonnes
Weight of base	550 tonnes (steel); 1320 tonnes (ballast)

TANKERS	
Number	1 (Medora), permanently moored offshore to provide 1.5×10^6 bbl of buffer storage ($\sim$ 8 days peak production)
Weight	210,000 tonnes deadweight

HUTTON

The Hutton field has estimated reserves of 24—34 million tonnes and was discovered in September 1973. Production is due to start in early 1984 and an eventual peak rate of 5.7 million tonnes/year is expected. The operating company, Conoco, intends to develop the field using a floating Tension Leg Platform (TLP); the platform will be anchored to tubular steel tethers pinned to the sea bed and a tension of approximately 1000 tonnes weight in each of the twelve mooring lines will eliminate vertical movement but allow a small degree of horizontal freedom. The TLP will be the first commercial application of its type in the world. Oil from the field will be piped to Amoco's North West Hutton field and thence into the Brent pipeline system.

HUTTON FIELD

GENERAL	
Name	Hutton
Location	Blocks 211/28 and 211/27
Operator	Conoco
Company interest	Block 211/28: Conoco Inc. (20%); BNOC (20%); Gulf Oil Corp. (20%) Block 211/27: Amoco (UK) Exploration Co. (10.31%); British Gas Council (10.31%); Mobil North Sea Ltd. (8%); Amerada Petroleum Corp. UK Ltd. (7.23%); North Sea Inc. (a subsidiary of Texas Eastern) (4.15%)
Discovery date	September 1973
Production date	Expected early 1984
Peak production rate	5.7×10^6 tonnes/year
Number of platforms	1 (Hutton)

ENVIRONMENT	
Water depth	147 m
Geological structure	Middle Jurassic "Brent Sand"
Dimension of geological structure	9.3 km (N–S) $\times$ 3.7 km (E–W)

DISCOVERY DRILLING	
Appraisal wells after discovery well	3
Total wells to determine viability	4 (including discovery well)

PRODUCTION DRILLING	
Total wells anticipated	32 (including reinjection wells which will form $\sim$ 50% of total)
Average expected depth	3048 m

RESERVES	
Crude oil	$23.8 \times 10^6 - 34 \times 10^6$ tonnes

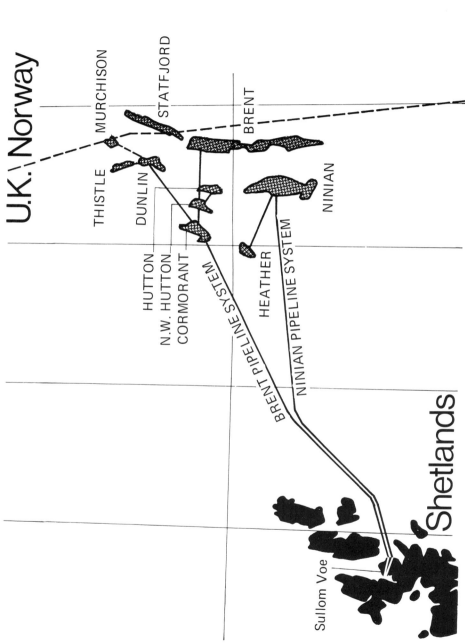

FIGURE 7.22 Map showing the location of Hutton field and details of the proposed connection with the Brent pipeline system. (By courtesy of Conoco.)

HUTTON PLATFORM

GENERAL	
Name	Hutton
Installation date	Expected late 1983
Type of jacket	Floating Tension Leg Platform (TLP)
Number of columns of TLP	8
Standard well conductors	32
Subsea well conductors	0
Production capacity	115,000 bbl/day
Storage capacity	0

SUBSTRUCTURE	
Tubular steel lines (mooring tethers)	12
Weight lines plus anchors	12,670 tonnes
Weight risers and mooring system	3750 tonnes
Weight ballast	1980 tonnes
Weight structural steel for TLP	22,040 tonnes
Total weight TLP (excluding deck, modules, and equipment)	22,040 tonnes

SUPERSTRUCTURE	
Weight of deck, modules, and equipment	16,530 tonnes

HUTTON ANCILLARY FACILITIES

OFFSHORE INTER-FIELD PIPELINES		
Function	*Outside diameter (in.)*	*Length (km)*
Oil: Hutton platform—North West Hutton	12.75	6.4

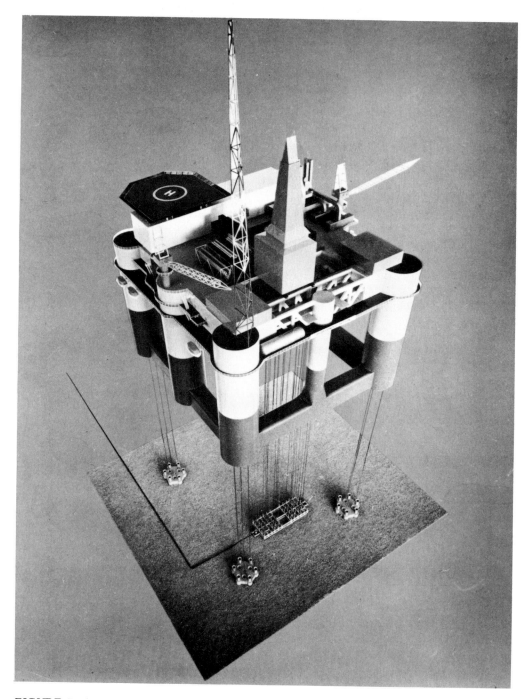

FIGURE 7.23 A scale model of the floating Tension Leg Platform (TLP) to be installed in Hutton field. (By courtesy of Conoco.)

MAGNUS

The Magnus field is located in the northernmost part of the U.K.sector.The field was discovered in March 1974 at a record North Sea water depth of 187 m (614 ft.) and its reserves are estimated as 60 million tonnes. The operating company, BP, will employ a self-floating steel platform and a series of pre-drilled wells to develop the field. Production is due to begin in 1983 and a peak rate of 125,000 barrels/day (equivalent to 5.9 million tonnes/year) is expected in 1984. Oil from the field will be transported by pipeline to Sullom Voe via the Ninian system. At the time of writing, the method to be used for transporting gas from the field is still undecided, pending the outcome of the Mobil/British Gas Corporation gas-gathering study.

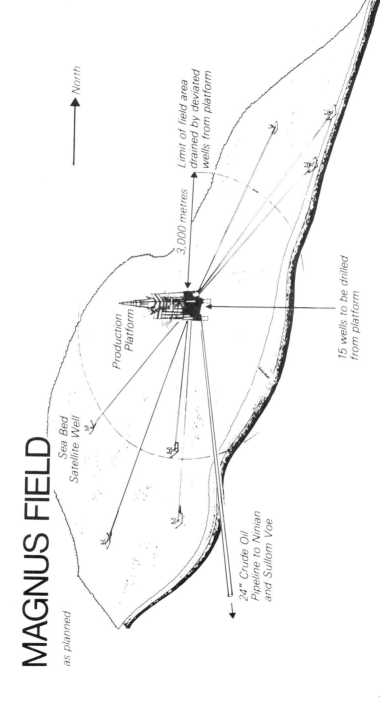

MAGNUS FIELD

as planned

↑ North

Sea Bed
Satellite Well

Production
Platform

3,000 metres

Limit of field area
drained by deviated
wells from platform

15 wells to be drilled
from platform

24" Crude Oil
Pipeline to Ninian
and Sullom Voe

FIGURE 7.24 Schematic diagram of Magnus field. (By courtesy of British Petroleum.)

MAGNUS FIELD

GENERAL	
Name	Magnus
Location	Block 211/12a
Operator	British Petroleum Ltd.
Company interest	British Petroleum Ltd. (100%)
Discovery date	March 1974
Production date	Expected 1983
Peak production rate	5.9×10^6 tonnes/year
API gravity of crude oil	39.3°
Number of platforms	1 (Magnus)

ENVIRONMENT	
Water depth	187 m
Geological structure	Middle and Upper Jurassic

DISCOVERY DRILLING	
Total wells to determine viability	11

PRODUCTION DRILLING	
Total wells anticipated (including reinjection wells)	22 (7 subsea; 15 from platform)
Average expected depth	2895 m

RESERVES	
Crude oil	60×10^6 tonnes

MAGNUS PLATFORM

GENERAL	
Name	Magnus
Installation date	Expected 1982
Jacket design	CJB—Earl and Wright Ltd.
Fabricating company	Highland Fabricators
Fabrication site	Nigg Bay, Scotland
Type of jacket	Steel, self-floating structure
Number of legs	4
Vertical height (from mud line to lowest deck)	211 m
Standard well conductors	20
Subsea well conductors	7 (4 production; 3 water injection)
Production capacity	125,000 bbl/day (oil); 50×10^6 scf/day (gas); 9000 bbl/day (natural-gas liquids)
Storage capacity	0
SUBSTRUCTURE	
Piles driven	36
Total weight steel for piles	12,240 tonnes
Weight structural steel for jacket	40,700 tonnes
Total weight jacket (excluding deck, modules, and equipment)	40,700 tonnes
SUPERSTRUCTURE	
Weight of deck, modules, and equipment	30,800 tonnes

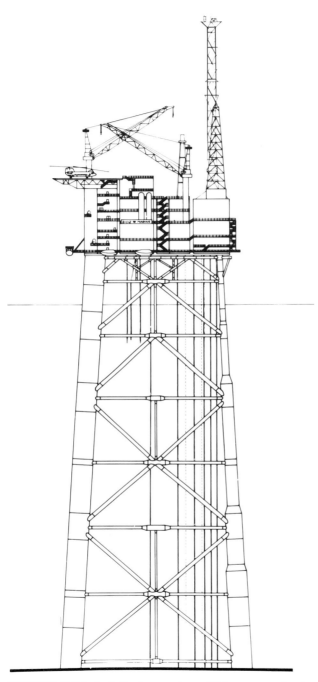

FIGURE 7.25 Artist's impression of Magnus production platform. (By courtesy of British Petroleum.)

184

MAGNUS ANCILLARY FACILITIES

OFFSHORE INTRA-FIELD PIPELINES		
Function	*Outside diameter (in.)*	*Length (km)*
7 flow lines to subsea wells	6	Various
Oil: Magnus platform—Ninian system	24	91.6

OFFSHORE INTER-FIELD PIPELINES		
Function	*Outside diameter (in.)*	*Length (km)*
Gas: will possibly be transferred to the Brent gas pipeline system, or to a new line resulting from the Mobil/ BGC gas-gathering study; the platform is being provided with a 20-in. diameter gas riser	Not yet known	

MAUREEN

Maureen field was discovered in February 1973 and is being developed by Phillips Petroleum; recoverable reserves are estimated as 21 million tonnes. Production wells are being pre-drilled using a sea-bed template, concurrently with the construction of the world's largest steel gravity platform which will be used to develop the field. The platform will have 650,000 barrels of internal storage capacity and an integrated deck, fully equipped and mated to the platform prior to tow-out. An Articulated Loading Column (ALC) will be used to load oil from the field into tankers; the ALC will be the first of its kind to be made of concrete. Production is expected to begin in 1981 or 1982, and an eventual peak rate of 4 million tonnes/year is anticipated.

MAUREEN FIELD

GENERAL	
Name	Maureen
Location	Block 16/29a
Operator	Phillips Petroleum
Company interest	Phillips Petroleum (33.78%); Fina Exploration Ltd. (28.96%); Agip UK Ltd. (17.26%); Century Power and Light Ltd. (9%); Ultramar Exploration Ltd. (6%); British Electric Traction Co. Ltd. (5%). Under the terms of a state participation agreement (signed April 1978) BNOC have an option to purchase up to 51% of each company's share of Maureen field production at current market prices
Discovery date	February 1973
Production date	Expected 1981/1982
Peak production rate	4.0×10^6 tonnes/year
API gravity of crude oil	$31.3-35.9°$
Number of platforms	1 (Maureen)

ENVIRONMENT	
Water depth	98 m
Geological structure	Paleocene sandstone

DISCOVERY DRILLING	
Appraisal wells after discovery well	3
Total wells to determine viability	4 (including discovery well)

PRODUCTION DRILLING	
Total wells anticipated	19 (12 production; 7 water injection)
Average expected depth	2469–3104 m

RESERVES	
Crude oil	21×10^6 tonnes

187

MAUREEN PLATFORM

GENERAL	
Name	Maureen
Installation date	Expected summer 1983
Platform design	Tecnomare
Fabricating company	Ayrshire Marine Constructors
Fabrication site	Hunterstone, Scotland
Building time (contract to installation)	36 months
Type of jacket	Steel(as of summer 1980, the largest proposed steel gravity platform in the world)
Number of legs	3
Standard well conductors	19
Subsea well conductors	0
Production capacity	70,000 bbl/day
Storage capacity	650,000 bbl(in legs of gravity platform)

SUBSTRUCTURE	
Weight structural steel for gravity platform	40,000 tonnes
Total weight gravity platform (excluding deck, modules, equipment, and drilling conductor)	40,000 tonnes
Weight solid ballast	51,000 tonnes (iron-ore aggregate)

SUPERSTRUCTURE	
Type of deck	Steel, integrated deck
Weight of deck, modules, and equipment	16,200 tonnes
Weight of drilling conductor	490 tonnes

FIGURE 7.26 Scale model of the world's largest proposed steel gravity platform, to be installed in Maureen field. (By courtesy of Phillips Petroleum.)

MAUREEN ANCILLARY FACILITIES

OFFSHORE INTRA-FIELD PIPELINES

Function	Outside diameter (in.)	Length (km)
Oil: Maureen platform—field terminal loading system	24	2.3

FIELD TERMINAL LOADING SYSTEM

Terminal construction	Concrete loading tower designed by Equipments Mechaniques et Hydrauliques for an Articulated Loading Column (ALC); built by Howard Doris Ltd., Loch Kishorn, Scotland
Storage capacity	0
Overall dimensions	89.9 m (height) $\times$ 9.1 m (diameter)
Loading capacity	20,000 bbl/hour maximum

TANKERS

Number	2 dedicated vessels
Weight	85,000—100,000 tonnes deadweight each

MONTROSE

The Montrose field, discovered in September 1969, was the first offshore oil field to be found in the North Sea area. The field contains estimated recoverable reserves of 12 million tonnes, and a peak production rate of 40,000 barrels/day (equivalent to 1.4 million tonnes/year) is expected in 1979/1980. The operating company, Amoco, has drilled twenty-four wells from a single steel production platform. Oil is transported from the field by tankers which are loaded at two Single-point Buoy Mooring (SBM) facilities.

One appraisal well has been drilled to date in the southern extension of the field (South Montrose). South Montrose is believed to have reserves of 4 million tonnes, and this additional oil could be produced economically from a small production platform linked to the main Montrose field facilities.

MONTROSE FIELD

GENERAL

Name	Montrose
Location	Blocks 22/17 and 22/18
Operator	Amoco UK
Company interest	Amoco (UK) Petroleum Ltd. (30.77%); British Gas Corp. (30.77%); Amerada (23.08%); Texas Eastern (15.38%)
Discovery date	September 1969
Production date	June 1976
Peak production rate	1.4×10^6 tonnes/year in 1979
API gravity of crude oil	$40.1°$
Number of platforms	1 (Montrose)

ENVIRONMENT

Water depth	90 m
Geological structure	Paleocene sandstone
Dimension of geological structure	62.2 km^2

DISCOVERY DRILLING

Dry wells before discovery well	0
Appraisal wells after discovery well	2
Total wells to determine viability	3 (including discovery well)

PRODUCTION DRILLING

Total wells anticipated	24 (including reinjection wells)
Average expected depth	3658 m

RESERVES

Crude oil	12×10^6 tonnes
Gas	Small quantities, used as fuel on platform

MONTROSE PLATFORM

GENERAL	
Name	Montrose
Installation date	August 1975
Fabricating company	Union Industrielle et d'Enterprise
Fabrication site	Le Havre, France
Building time (contract to installation)	11 months
Type of jacket	Steel
Number of legs	8
Standard well conductors	24
Subsea well conductors	Possible subsea wells or a small additional drilling platform to complete southern lobe of reservoir
Production capacity	60,000 bbl/day
Storage capacity	0

SUBSTRUCTURE	
Piles driven	38 (includes 6 for flare bridge support)
Average depth driven	46 m
Total weight steel for piles	2300 tonnes
Weight structural steel for jacket	6500 tonnes
Total weight jacket (excluding deck, modules, and equipment)	6500 tonnes

SUPERSTRUCTURE	
Type of deck	2 steel decks with tanks
Weight of deck	1600 tonnes total
Weight of modules and equipment	4486 tonnes

FIGURE 7.27 Montrose platform. (By courtesy of Amoco U.K. Petroleum Ltd.)

MONTROSE ANCILLARY FACILITIES

OFFSHORE INTRA-FIELD PIPELINES		
Function	*Outside diameter (in.)*	*Length (km)*
Oil: lines to "SBMs" (see below)	10	1.6 total

FIELD TERMINAL LOADING SYSTEM	
Terminal construction	2 Single Buoy Moorings (SBM)
Storage capacity	0
Weight of steel	400 tonnes
Total weight	400 tonnes

TANKERS	
Number	2
Weight	72,000 tonnes deadweight each

REMOTE VENT/FLARE	
Flare construction	Steel, supported by tripod steel support
Weight of steel	1260 tonnes
Total weight	1260 tonnes

MURCHISON

Murchison field was discovered in September 1975 and has estimated reserves of 51 million tonnes of oil. The field is located on the border of the U.K. and Norwegian sectors, in a water depth of 156 m. The world's largest steel jacket was installed in the field in August 1979; twenty-two production wells will be drilled from the jacket and three subsea wells will be connected to it. The Murchison jacket was also the largest steel framework ever launched from a barge. The operating company, Conoco, expects production to begin during the summer of 1980, with a peak rate of 7.2 million tonnes/year (including production from the Norwegian sector) being reached in 1982. The oil will be transported by pipeline to the Dunlin platform and then on to Sullom Voe.

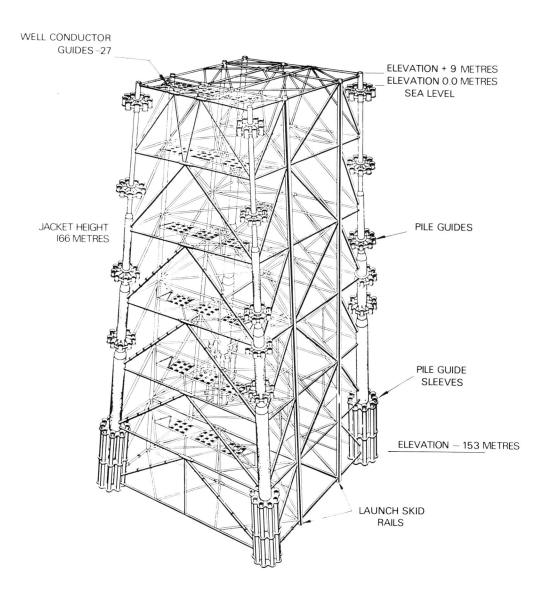

WELL CONDUCTOR
GUIDES -27

ELEVATION + 9 METRES
ELEVATION 0.0 METRES
SEA LEVEL

JACKET HEIGHT
166 METRES

PILE GUIDES

PILE GUIDE
SLEEVES

ELEVATION — 153 METRES

LAUNCH SKID
RAILS

FIGURE 7.28 Artist's impression of Murchison jacket. (By courtesy of Conoco.)

197

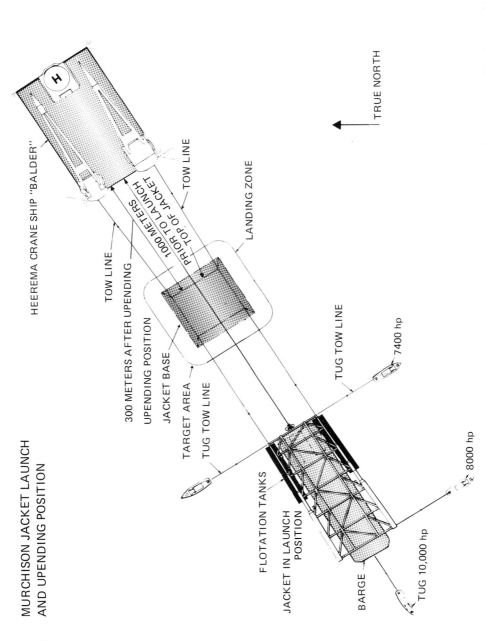

FIGURE 7.29 The installation of Murchison jacket: Phase I, launching the jacket from its barge and positioning it prior to upending. (By courtesy of Conoco.)

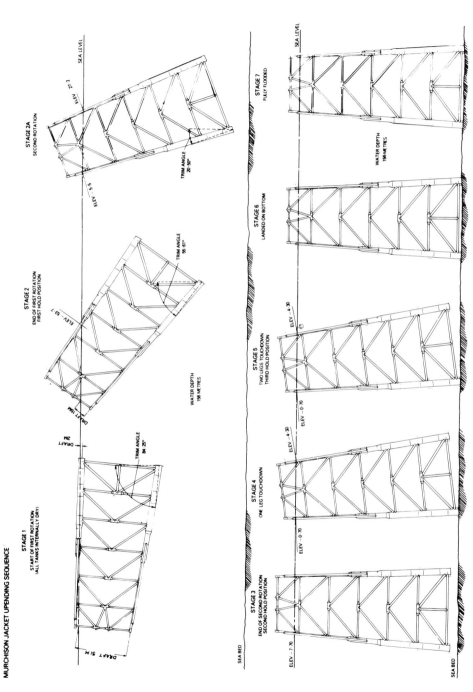

FIGURE 7.30 The installation of Murchison jacket: Phase II, upending the jacket and positioning it on the sea bed. (By courtesy of Conoco.)

199

MURCHISON FIELD

GENERAL

Name	Murchison
Location	Blocks 211/19 (UK) and 33/9 (Norway)
Operator	Conoco North Sea Inc.
Company interest	UK Block 211/19: Conoco (33.3%); BNOC Exploration Ltd. (33.3%); Gulf Oil Corp. (33.3%). Norwegian Block 33/9: Statoil (50%); Mobil Exploration Norway Inc. (15%); Conoco Norway Inc. (10%); Esso Exploration and Production Norway (10%); A/S Norske Shell (10%); Saga Petroleum A/S (1.88%); Amerada Petroleum Corp. Norway (1.04%); Amoco Norway Oil Co.(1.04%); Texas Eastern Norway Inc. (1.04%)
Discovery date	September 1975
Production date	Summer 1980
Peak production rate	7.2×10^6 tonnes/year (including production from Norwegian block)
API gravity of crude oil	37°
Number of platforms	1 (Murchison)

ENVIRONMENT

Water depth	156 m
Geological structure	Middle Jurassic "Brent Sand"
Dimension of geological structure	Overall thickness 122 m, of which 91 m is oil-bearing sands; deposits at average depth of 3018 m

DISCOVERY DRILLING

Appraisal wells after discovery well (including any dry wells)	2
Total wells to determine viability (including discovery well)	3

MURCHISON FIELD (continued)

PRODUCTION DRILLING	
Total wells anticipated (including reinjection wells)	25 (10 oil production; 10 water injection; 2 gas injection; 3 subsea wells drilled earlier for discovery and appraisal, of which 2 oil production and 1 water injection)
Average expected depth	3018 m

RESERVES	
Crude oil	51×10^6 tonnes (including reserves in Norwegian block)

MURCHISON PLATFORM

GENERAL	
Name	Murchison
Installation date	August 1979
Fabricating company	McDermott
Fabrication site	Ardersier, Scotland
Building time (contract to installation)	~ 24 months
Type of jacket	Steel, drilling and production
Number of legs	4
Vertical height (from mud line to lowest deck)	166 m
Standard well conductors	27
Subsea well conductors	3
Production capacity	150,000 bbl/day
Storage capacity	0

SUBSTRUCTURE	
Piles driven	32 (tubular steel)
Total weight steel for piles	8544 tonnes
Weight basic structure	18,900 tonnes
Weight auxiliary equipment	1400 tonnes
Total weight jacket (excluding deck, modules, and equipment)	20,300 tonnes

SUPERSTRUCTURE	
Type of deck	Steel, tubular module-support frame
Weight of deck	5000 tonnes
Weight of modules and equipment	24,000 tonnes (14 modules plus drilling rig and flare boom)

MURCHISON ANCILLARY FACILITIES

OFFSHORE INTER-FIELD PIPELINES		
Function	Outside diameter (in.)	Length (km)
Oil: Murchison platform—Dunlin	16	16

NINIAN

The Ninian field was discovered in January 1974 and production began in December 1978. It is the third-largest U.K. offshore oil field, with recoverable reserves of 155 million tonnes and an anticipated peak production rate of 17.7 million tonnes/year in 1981. Chevron Petroleum, the operating company, has employed one concrete and two steel platforms in the development of the field. Ninian Central is the largest concrete platform (356,000 tonnes) to be installed in the U.K. sector. The oil from the Ninian field is transported ashore using a pipeline to Sullom Voe. During 1980 development drilling continued from all three platforms.

NINIAN FIELD

GENERAL	
Name	Ninian
Location	Blocks 3/3 and 3/8a
Operator	Chevron Petroleum Co. Ltd.
Company interest	BNOC (30%); ICI Petroleum Ltd. (26%); Chevron Petroleum Co. Ltd. (24%); Murphy Petroleum (10%); Ocean Exploration (10%)
Discovery date	January 1974
Production date	December 1978
Peak production rate	17.7×10^6 tonnes/year in 1981
API gravity of crude oil	$35.1°$
Number of platforms	3 (Ninian Southern, Central, Northern)
ENVIRONMENT	
Water depth	140.2 m
Geological structure	Middle and Lower Jurassic (sediments)
Dimension of geological structure	Pear shaped, 9.7×17.7 km^2
DISCOVERY DRILLING	
Dry wells before discovery well	0
Appraisal wells after discovery well	7
Total wells to determine viability	8 (including discovery well)
PRODUCTION DRILLING	
Total wells anticipated	96 (including reinjection wells)
Average expected depth	4084 m
RESERVES	
Crude oil	155×10^6 tonnes

NINIAN SOUTHERN PLATFORM

GENERAL	
Name	Ninian Southern
Installation date	June 1977
Fabricating company	Highland Fabricators
Fabrication site	Nigg Bay, Scotland
Type of jacket	Steel
Number of legs	4
Vertical height (from mud line to lowest deck)	165 m
Standard well conductors	42
Subsea well conductors	0
Production capacity	140,000 bbl/day
Storage capacity	0

SUBSTRUCTURE	
Piles driven	32 (each $1.8 \times 0.062 \times 80$ m^3)
Average depth driven	50 m
Total weight steel for piles	8000 tonnes
Weight structural steel for jacket	20,000 tonnes
Total weight jacket (excluding deck, modules, and equipment)	20,000 tonnes

SUPERSTRUCTURE	
Type of deck	Steel, truss deck integrated with modules
Weight of deck	0 (integral part of tower structure)
Weight of modules and equipment	17,497 tonnes

FIGURE 7.31 Ninian Southern platform. (By courtesy of Chevron Petroleum Ltd.)

207

NINIAN CENTRAL PLATFORM

GENERAL	
Name	Ninian Central
Installation date	May 1978
Fabricating company	Howard Doris Ltd.
Fabrication site	Loch Kishorn, Scotland
Type of jacket	Concrete
Vertical height (from mud line to lowest deck)	169.5 m
Standard well conductors	42
Subsea well conductors	0
Production capacity	140,000 bbl/day
Storage capacity	1,100,000 bbl seawater ballast

SUBSTRUCTURE	
Weight structural steel for jacket	10,000 tonnes
Weight reinforcing steel for jacket	30,000 tonnes
Total weight concrete for jacket	356,000 tonnes
Total volume concrete for jacket	150,000 m^3
Total weight jacket (excluding deck, modules, equipment, and ballast)	396,000 tonnes
Weight ballast	217,000 tonnes

SUPERSTRUCTURE	
Type of deck	Steel
Weight of deck	15,000 tonnes
Weight of modules and equipment	45,000 tonnes

NINIAN NORTHERN PLATFORM

GENERAL	
Name	Ninian Northern
Installation date	July 1978
Fabricating company	Highlands Fabricators
Fabrication site	Nigg Bay, Scotland
Type of jacket	Steel
Number of legs	4
Vertical height (from mud line to lowest deck)	165.5 m
Standard well conductors	24
Subsea well conductors	0
Production capacity	81,000 bbl/day
Storage capacity	0

SUBSTRUCTURE	
Piles driven	26
Average depth driven	50 m
Total weight steel for piles	6000 tonnes
Weight structural steel for jacket	17,000 tonnes
Total weight jacket (excluding deck, modules, and equipment)	17,000 tonnes

SUPERSTRUCTURE	
Type of deck	Steel, truss deck integrated with modules
Weight of deck	0 (integral part of tower structure)
Weight of modules and equipment	9000 tonnes

NINIAN ANCILLARY FACILITIES

OFFSHORE INTRA-FIELD PIPELINES		
Function	*Outside diameter (in.)*	*Length (km)*
Oil: Ninian Southern—Ninian Central	24	4.02
FIELD-TO-SHORE PIPELINES		
Function	*Outside diameter (in.)*	*Length (km)*
Oil: Ninian—Sullom Voe, Shetlands	36	168.98

NORTH CORMORANT

North Cormorant was discovered in July 1974. With estimated reserves of 55 million tonnes, it is one of the larger fields under development in the U.K. sector and an eventual peak production rate of 7.3 million tonnes/year is expected. The operating companies, Shell and Esso, intend to install a fixed-leg steel platform in 1981 and production is due to start in 1982. Oil from the field will be transferred into the Brent network and gas will be transported using the South Cormorant—Brent gas-pipeline system.

NORTH CORMORANT FIELD

GENERAL	
Name	North Cormorant
Location	Block 211/21a
Operator	Shell/Esso
Company interest	Shell (50%); Esso (50%)
Discovery date	July 1974
Production date	Expected 1982
Peak production rate	7.3×10^6 tonnes/year
API gravity of crude oil	35°
Number of platforms	1 (North Cormorant)

ENVIRONMENT	
Water depth	160 m
Geological structure	Middle Jurassic
Dimension of geological structure	10×4 km^2

DISCOVERY DRILLING	
Total wells to determine viability	6

PRODUCTION DRILLING	
Total wells anticipated (including reinjection wells)	32 (21 production; 11 water injection)
Average expected depth	2743 m

RESERVES	
Crude oil	55×10^6 tonnes

NORTH CORMORANT PLATFORM

GENERAL	
Name	North Cormorant
Installation date	Expected April 1981
Fabricating company	Redpath de Groot Caledonian and Union Industrielle et d'Enterprise
Fabrication site	Methil, Scotland and Cherbourg, France
Building time (contract to installation)	24 months
Type of jacket	Steel
Number of legs	8
Standard well conductors	40
Subsea well conductors	Possibly 2 satellite wells (1 water injection in northern part of reservoir; 1 production in southern part); a 4-well manifold for water injection may also be needed
Production capacity	180,000 bbl/day
Storage capacity	0

SUBSTRUCTURE	
Piles driven	28
Total weight steel for piles	6100 tonnes
Weight structural steel for jacket	21,300 tonnes
Total weight jacket (excluding deck, modules, and equipment)	21,300 tonnes

SUPERSTRUCTURE	
Type of deck	Steel, module-support frame
Weight of deck	1800 tonnes
Weight of modules and equipment	44,467 tonnes

NORTH CORMORANT ANCILLARY FACILITIES

OFFSHORE INTER-FIELD PIPELINES		
Function	*Outside diameter (in.)*	*Length (km)*
Oil: North Cormorant—South Cormorant A	20	17
Gas: North Cormorant—South Cormorant A	10	22.1

NORTH WEST HUTTON

North West Hutton field was discovered in April 1975 and is being developed by Amoco. Recoverable reserves are estimated as 37.5 million tonnes, making the field small-to-medium sized by North Sea standards. Development plans approved in 1979 by the U.K. Department of Energy include provision for a single fixed platform which will be placed over a drilling template positioned earlier. The semi-submersible rig *Ventura 1* was contracted in 1979 for the installation of the template and pre-drilling of eight production wells, to facilitate early production from the field. Production is expected to start in 1982, with an eventual peak rate of 5.1 million tonnes/year. Oil from the field will be transported by pipeline to South Cormorant A platform and the gas produced will be routed along a spur to join Shell/Esso's Welgas export pipeline.

NORTH WEST HUTTON FIELD

GENERAL	
Name	North West Hutton
Location	Block 211/27
Operator	Amoco UK
Company interest	Amoco UK (25.77%); Gas Council Exploration Ltd. (25.77%); Mobil North Sea Ltd. (20%); Amerada Petroleum Corp. UK Ltd. (18.08%); Texas Eastern (10.38%)
Discovery date	April 1975
Production date	Expected 1982
Peak production rate	5.1×10^6 tonnes/year (crude oil)
API gravity of crude oil	$37°$
Number of platforms	1 (North West Hutton)

ENVIRONMENT	
Water depth	144 m
Geological structure	Middle Jurassic
Dimension of geological structure	35 km^2

DISCOVERY DRILLING	
Appraisal wells after discovery well	6
Total wells to determine viability	7 (including discovery well)

PRODUCTION DRILLING	
Total wells anticipated	30 (20 production; 10 water injection)
Average expected depth	4000 m

RESERVES	
Crude oil	37.5×10^6 tonnes
Gas	120×10^9 scf

NORTH WEST HUTTON PLATFORM

GENERAL	
Name	North West Hutton
Installation date	Expected summer/autumn 1982
Fabricating company	McDermott
Fabrication site	Ardersier, Scotland
Type of jacket	Steel platform placed over drilling template positioned earlier
Number of legs	4
Vertical height (from mud line to lowest deck)	152 m
Standard well conductors	40
Subsea well conductors	0
Production capacity	100,000 bbl/day (oil); 35×10^6 scf/day (gas)
Storage capacity	0

SUBSTRUCTURE	
Piles driven	20
Average depth driven	70 m
Total weight steel for piles	6500 tonnes
Weight drilling conductor	230 tonnes
Weight structural steel for jacket	16,000 tonnes
Total weight jacket (excluding deck, modules, and equipment)	16,000 tonnes

SUPERSTRUCTURE	
Type of deck	Steel, module-support frame
Weight of deck	1372 tonnes
Weight of modules and equipment	25,700 tonnes

NORTH WEST HUTTON ANCILLARY FACILITIES

OFFSHORE INTER-FIELD PIPELINES		
Function	*Outside diameter (in.)*	*Length (km)*
Oil: North West Hutton platform— South Cormorant A	20	12
Gas: North West Hutton platform— Welgas line (Shell/Esso)	10	15

PIPER

The Piper field, discovered in January 1973, is a reasonably large field with recoverable reserves of 88 million tonnes. Occidental Petroleum, the operating company, has developed the field using a single steel platform, and a development drilling program of twenty-six wells was completed in 1979. Piper has continued to perform better than originally expected with peak production rates of 285,000–300,000 barrels/day ($\sim$ 12.6 million tonnes/year) achieved in 1978/1979. The oil produced is transported by pipeline to the Flotta terminal and gas is delivered through a pipeline link to the Frigg manifold compression platform.

PIPER FIELD

GENERAL	
Name	Piper
Location	Block 15/17
Operator	Occidental Petroleum (UK) Ltd.
Company interest	Occidental Petroleum (UK) Ltd. (36.5%); Getty Oil (Britain) Ltd. (23.5%); Allied Chemical (GB) Ltd. (20%); Thomson North Sea Ltd. (20%)
Discovery date	January 1973
Production date	December 1976
Peak production rate	12.6×10^6 tonnes/year in 1979
API gravity of crude oil	$36°$
Number of platforms	1 (Piper)

ENVIRONMENT	
Water depth	121.9 m
Geological structure	Upper and Middle Jurassic (volcanics)
Dimension of geological structure	Approximately circular, diameter 8.4 km

DISCOVERY DRILLING	
Dry wells before discovery well	3 (third well abandoned at 457 m)
Appraisal wells after discovery well	5 (1 abandoned at 1219 m)
Total wells to determine viability	9 (including discovery well)

PRODUCTION DRILLING	
Total wells anticipated	26 (including reinjection wells)
Average expected depth	2896 m

RESERVES	
Crude oil	88×10^6 tonnes

PIPER PLATFORM

GENERAL	
Name	Piper
Installation date	June 1975
Fabricating company	McDermott and Union Industrielle et d'Enterprise
Fabrication site	Ardersier, Scotland and Le Havre, France
Building time (contract to installation)	28 months
Type of jacket	Steel
Number of legs	8
Vertical height (from mud line to lowest deck)	150.9 m
Standard well conductors	36
Subsea well conductors	Under consideration
Production capacity	250,000 bbl/day
Storage capacity	0

SUBSTRUCTURE	
Piles driven	28 (4 erection; 24 primary)
Average depth driven	38.7 m
Piles drilled	24
Average depth drilled	33.5 m
Total weight steel for piles	8016 tonnes
Weight structural steel for jacket	12,972 tonnes
Total weight jacket (excluding deck, modules, and equipment)	12,972 tonnes

FIGURE 7.32 Piper production platform. (By courtesy of Occidental Petroleum.)

PIPER PLATFORM (continued)

SUPERSTRUCTURE	
Type of deck	Steel
Weight of deck	1089 tonnes
Weight of modules and equipment	5715 tonnes

PIPER ANCILLARY FACILITIES

FIELD-TO-SHORE PIPELINES		
Function	*Outside diameter (in.)*	*Length (km)*
Oil: Piper—Flotta, Orkneys (line shared with Claymore)	30	199.5

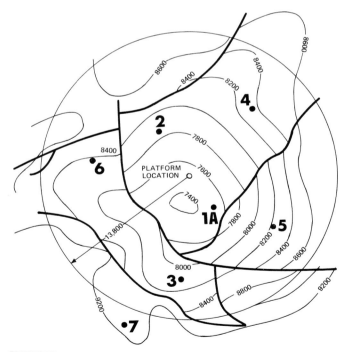

FIGURE 7.33 Geological strata in Piper field.

SOUTH CORMORANT

South Cormorant, discovered in September 1972 and operated by Shell, is a small field with recoverable reserves of only 12 million tonnes. Production began in December 1979 from two wells drilled from a single concrete platform, South Cormorant A, installed in May 1978. A peak production rate of 3 million tonnes/year is expected in 1982. Oil from the field is transported by pipeline to Sullom Voe.

South Cormorant A platform is a central point in the Brent pipeline system. All crude oil transported to the Brent system is gathered at South Cormorant A platform and then transferred 155 km via a 36-in. pipeline to Sullom Voe. The platform will eventually gather oil produced from the Brent, Dunlin, North and South Cormorant, Thistle, Hutton, and North West Hutton fields.

FIGURE 7.34 South Cormorant A platform. (By courtesy of Shell U.K. Ltd.)

SOUTH CORMORANT FIELD

GENERAL	
Name	South Cormorant
Location	Blocks 211/26a and 211/21a
Operator	Shell (UK) Ltd.
Company interest	Shell (50%); Esso (50%)
Discovery date	September 1972
Production date	December 1979
Peak production rate	3×10^6 tonnes/year in 1982
Number of platforms	1 (South Cormorant A)

ENVIRONMENT	
Water depth	149 m
Geological structure	Middle Jurassic
Dimension of geological structure	50 km^2

DISCOVERY DRILLING	
Dry wells before discovery well	0
Appraisal wells after discovery well (including any dry wells)	2
Total wells to determine viability (including discovery well)	3

PRODUCTION DRILLING	
Total wells anticipated (including reinjection wells)	22 (16 from platform; 6 subsea, of which 1 previously drilled)
Average expected depth	3048 m

RESERVES	
Crude oil	12×10^6 tonnes (block 211/26a only)

SOUTH CORMORANT A PLATFORM

GENERAL	
Name	South Cormorant A
Installation date	May 1978
Fabricating company	McAlpine/Sea Tank
Fabrication site	Ardyne Point, Scotland
Building time (contract to installation)	48 months
Type of jacket	Concrete
Number of legs	4
Vertical height (from mud line to lowest deck)	172.2 m
Standard well conductors	36
Subsea well conductors	0
Production capacity	60,000 bbl/day (oil); 30×10^6 scf/day (gas)
Storage capacity	1,000,000 bbl

SUBSTRUCTURE	
Weight reinforcing steel for jacket	13,500 tonnes
Weight prestressed steel for jacket	1000 tonnes
Total weight concrete for jacket	275,500 tonnes
Total volume concrete for jacket	115,000 m³
Total weight jacket (excluding deck, modules, and equipment)	290,000 tonnes

SUPERSTRUCTURE	
Type of deck	Steel, box girder (constructed in France and towed to Ardyne Point)
Weight of deck	4500 tonnes
Weight of modules and equipment	13,000 tonnes

SOUTH CORMORANT ANCILLARY FACILITIES

FIELD-TO-SHORE PIPELINES		
Function	*Outside diameter (in.)*	*Length (km)*
Oil: South Cormorant—Sullom Voe, Shetlands (shared line carrying oil from South Cormorant, Brent, Dunlin, Murchison, and Thistle fields)	36	150

TARTAN

Tartan field, which is being developed by Texaco, was discovered in December 1974. The field has recoverable reserves of 27 million tonnes and an eventual peak production rate of 4 million tonnes/year is expected. A single steel platform was installed in the summer of 1979; the first production wells were drilled during 1980 and production of oil is due to begin towards the end of 1980. Oil from the field will be transported by pipeline to Flotta via the Claymore system and gas will be transferred to St. Fergus via the Piper system.

TARTAN FIELD

GENERAL	
Name	Tartan
Location	Block 15/16
Operator	Texaco
Company interest	Texaco (100%)
Discovery date	December 1974
Production date	1980
Peak production rate	4.0×10^6 tonnes/year
API gravity of crude oil	$37°$
Number of platforms	1 (Tartan A)

ENVIRONMENT	
Water depth	142 m
Geological structure	Upper Jurassic (faulted ridge)
Dimension of geological structure	36.4 km^2

DISCOVERY DRILLING	
Total wells to determine viability (including discovery well)	9

PRODUCTION DRILLING	
Total wells anticipated (including reinjection wells)	30 (24 production; 6 to replace exploration wells, for additional production, or for water injection)
Average expected depth	3048–3658 m

RESERVES	
Crude oil	27×10^6 tonnes

FIGURE 7.36 Thistle production platform. (By courtesy of BNOC Development.)

235

THISTLE FIELD

GENERAL	
Name	Thistle
Location	Blocks 211/18a and 211/19a
Operator	BNOC Development
Company interest	Deminex (UK) Exploration and Production Ltd. (22.5%); Deminex Oil and Gas (UK) (20%); Santa Fe (UK) Ltd. (16.9%); BNOC Development (15.6%); Tricentrol Thistle Development Ltd. (10%); Burmah Oil (Exploration) Ltd. (8.4%); BNOC (Alpha) Ltd. (2.8%); Charterhouse Oil and Gas Ltd. (1.4%); Glenworth Property Ltd. (1.4%); Charterhouse Petroleum Development (1%)
Discovery date	July 1973
Production date	February 1978
Peak production rate	8.7×10^6 tonnes/year in 1982
API gravity of crude oil	$38.6°$
Number of platforms	1 (Thistle)

ENVIRONMENT	
Water depth	161.5 m
Geological structure	Middle Jurassic
Dimension of geological structure	16.1 km^2

DISCOVERY DRILLING	
Dry wells before discovery well	0
Appraisal wells after discovery well	5
Total wells to determine viability	6 (including discovery well)

PRODUCTION DRILLING	
Total wells anticipated	61 (including reinjection wells)
Average expected depth	3048–4877 m

THISTLE FIELD (continued)

RESERVES	
Crude oil	69×10^6 tonnes

THISTLE PLATFORM

GENERAL	
Name	Thistle
Installation date	August 1976
Fabricating company	Laing Offshore
Fabrication site	Teesside, England
Building time (construction time only)	11 months
Type of jacket	Steel
Number of legs	4
Vertical height	184.7 m (mud line—lowest deck)
Standard well conductors	60
Subsea well conductors	10
Production capacity	200,000 bbl/day
Storage capacity	70,000 bbl (integrated storage in jacket)

SUBSTRUCTURE	
Piles driven	42
Average depth driven	30.5 m
Piles drilled	34
Depth drilled	Up to 126.5 m
Total weight steel for piles	13,000 tonnes
Weight structural steel for jacket	31,650 tonnes
Total weight jacket (excluding deck, modules, and equipment)	31,650 tonnes (including ballast controls, risers, and integrated storage tanks)

THISTLE PLATFORM (continued)

SUPERSTRUCTURE	
Type of deck	Steel, box-girder skid-beams integrated into jacket
Weight of modules and equipment	25,930 tonnes

THISTLE ANCILLARY FACILITIES

OFFSHORE INTRA-FIELD PIPELINES		
Function	*Outside diameter (in.)*	*Length (km)*
Oil: Thistle platform—"SALM" (see below)	16	2.4

OFFSHORE INTER-FIELD PIPELINES		
Function	*Outside diameter (in.)*	*Length (km)*
Oil: Thistle platform—Dunlin A	16	11.26

FIELD TERMINAL LOADING SYSTEM	
Terminal construction	Single Anchor Leg Mooring (SALM)
Storage capacity	0
Weight of steel	905 tonnes
Weight of concrete	300 tonnes
Weight of ballast	2000 tonnes
Total weight	3205 tonnes

FIGURE 7.37 Tanker loading from the Single Anchor Leg Mooring (SALM) facility in Thistle field. (By courtesy of BNOC Development.)

8 SUMMARY

The exploration and development of the North Sea oil fields has been rapid. The first exploration wells were drilled in 1964 and the first major oil discovery was made in 1969; by 1980, in the U.K. sector alone, 14 fields (including Statfjord) were already in production with another 11 at various stages of development. The United Kingdom is now expected to achieve self sufficiency in crude oil by the end of 1980.

The development of these offshore fields has been a difficult and complex task, and, particularly because of the great water depths and the adverse weather conditions in the area, has demanded a large investment of natural and human resources. The research described in earlier chapters of this book set out to evaluate the resources (water, energy, land, manpower, and materials) needed to construct and operate the exploration, production, and transport facilities used in the U.K. sector; from this information the total direct resource requirements for the development of 23* of the fields in the U.K. sector were calculated.

A review of the facilities in July 1980 produced the following statistics. 602 exploration, 256 appraisal, and 629 production wells had been drilled in the area; at the same date it was anticipated that a further 947 wells would eventually be needed in the fields in production or under development. A total of 950 miles (1529 km)** of major crude-oil pipelines had been constructed or were under construction, together with 70 miles (113 km) of intrafield pipelines. 29 production platforms, 22 of them steel and 7 concrete, had been installed and a further 6 steel platforms were at various stages of construction or installation. If we include the Statfjord field, which lies on the border of the U.K. and Norwegian sectors, 14 fields were in production and another 11 were under development. 77.9 million tonnes (572 million barrels) of crude oil were produced in 1979, and forecasts for 1980 indicated a probable annual output of 80–85 million tonnes (587–624 million barrels).

The major expenditures of direct resources during field development occur during the phases of exploration- and appraisal-well drilling, platform and pipeline construction, and production-well drilling. Table 8.1 shows the total direct resources needed for construction in each of these phases of development; the resource requirements for marine seismic surveying and the construction of offshore loading facilities and remote flare vents are less significant and are not included here, although they are analyzed in detail in Chapter 6.

---

*As explained on page 7, the Statfjord and Heather fields were not included in the analysis.
**Including the Ekofisk–Teesside pipeline, which originates in the Norwegian sector but runs for most of its length through the U.K. sector.

TABLE 8.1 Total direct construction requirements for the major phases of field development.

Resource (units)	Requirements for the construction of			
	Exploration wells	Platforms	Pipelines	Production wells
Water ($\times 10^5$ m^3)	33	49	4	200
Energy ($\times 10^5$ GJ)[a]	347	1501	303	2244
Land (km^2)[b]	1	11	1	2
Labor ($\times 10^3$ man-years)	21	249	17	41
Materials ($\times 10^3$ tonnes)	285	2972	1031	1732

[a] All direct energy requirements, including electricity, are given here in units of GJ. Values originally in GJe were multiplied by 3 before inclusion in energy totals, based on an assumed generating efficiency of 33%.
[b] Temporary onshore land requirements for storage of equipment and materials, and for offices and docks, but excluding areas occupied on the sea bed.

The total weight of material and fuel-energy resources needed to construct the facilities in the U.K. sector is 18.5 million tonnes. Fuel-energy resources comprise 12.4 million tonnes of this total and construction and consumable materials account for the remaining 6.1 million tonnes. To gain some idea of the scale of these quantities, the structural steel required for the platforms alone (1.2 million tonnes) is equivalent to 173 Eiffel Towers. Figure 8.1 gives an overall view of the amounts and types of material required in the development of the fields.

In addition to the fuel-energy and material resources described above, 29.6 million tonnes of fresh and sea water are required during the development of the fields. Demands on manpower are also heavy: it is expected that, by 1985, 333,000 man-years of direct labor will have been expended.

The total direct energy required to develop the fields in the U.K. sector is estimated as 4761×10^5 GJ; the corresponding indirect and capital requirements are 1511×10^5 GJ and 1010×10^5 GJ, respectively. When the energy required for production and transport of the oil is included, we arrive at a total overall energy requirement* of 0.8122 GJ per tonne of crude oil produced and delivered to the refineries. Since this figure represents only 1.85% of the calorific value of the oil produced it can be seen that the expenditure of energy resources in developing and operating the North Sea fields produced a very high energy return. The return on "energy expenditure" is rapid: based on an estimated peak production rate of 115 million tonnes/year, the pay-back period is only 33 days.

The major design criteria for the steel or concrete platforms used in the U.K. sector appear to be water depth at the platform site and the number of well conductors required. There is little direct correlation between the total weights of the platforms and such factors as production rates and geographical position. For example, some of the heavier platforms have relatively low production rates, whereas a number of light concrete platforms have proportionally higher production rates and are situated in fairly remote deep-water areas. When comparing the resources required to construct either concrete or steel platforms, no significant differences are found. The concrete platform is slightly more demanding in terms of material requirements, but has the advantage of providing internal crude-oil storage capacity; the latter feature makes the concrete platform a viable alternative for more-remote locations where there is no direct access to an export pipeline.

There is still a wide variation in the published estimates of the ultimate recoverable reserves of oil under the North Sea. The various problems of reserve and resource estimation were discussed in Chapter 3, and a historical review of the changing estimates for the U.K. and Norwegian sectors was presented. It appears that it is still too early in the production phase to estimate the ultimate recoverable reserves with a low margin of error; the final amount of oil recovered will depend heavily upon the appreciation factor, the recovery rate, future discoveries, and the question of whether secondary or tertiary production methods will be employed. Suffice it to say that the amounts involved are more than significant with respect to the national demands of the United Kingdom and Norway.

Secondary production methods, involving the injection of pressurized water or gas into the oil-bearing formations, are either in use or will be used in practically all of the U.K.-sector

---

*Based on an estimated cumulative recovery of 1393.9 million tonnes of crude oil over the entire production lifetime of the area.

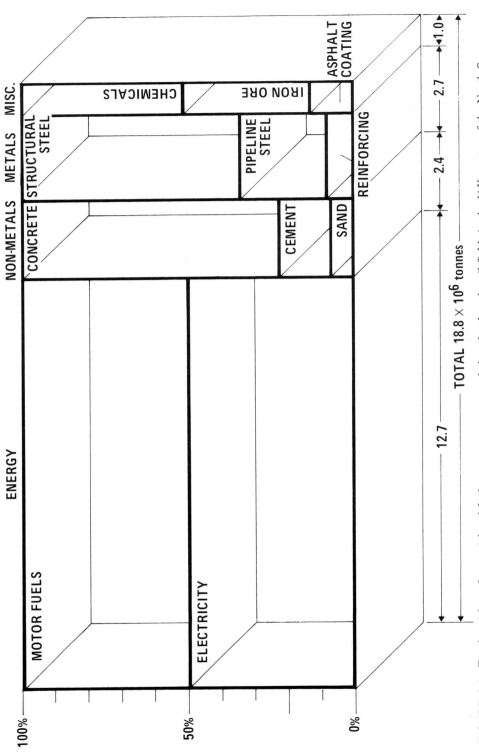

FIGURE 8.1 Total weights of material and fuel-energy resources needed to develop the oil fields in the U.K. sector of the North Sea. The pay-back periods for the fuel-energy resources are based on an estimated peak production rate of 115 million tonnes/year of crude oil.

fields; the energy needed for this form of production is about 1.2 times that required for primary production. From the results of this study, tertiary (or "enhanced") methods, in this case involving chemical injection, appear worthy of detailed consideration. The energy required may range from 3.4 to 5.1 times that needed for primary production but this still represents only 10% of the calorific value of the oil recovered. Furthermore, tertiary methods could be expected to produce an additional 50 million–200 million tonnes of crude oil.

Finally, the comparison between the natural gas produced from the Leman field and the crude oil produced from the U.K.-sector fields has yielded the following results. More units of energy are returned for a unit of energy expended in the Leman gas field than in the U.K.-sector oil fields studied. Also, more units of energy are returned per unit of water, manpower, or materials expended in the gas field than in the oil fields. Therefore it can be seen that the overall return on resources expended has been higher for Leman than for the 23 oil fields studied. However, it should be stressed that Leman is a major gas field in the southern part of the U.K. sector, whereas the 23 oil fields all lie in the middle and northern parts of the sector. It is therefore probable that the larger resource requirements for the oil fields can be attributed in large part to the greater water depths, more adverse weather conditions, and isolation of the more northerly areas.

REFERENCES

1   M. Grenon and B. Lapillone, The WELMM Approach to Energy Strategies and Options. RR-76-19. International Institute for Applied Systems Analysis, Laxenburg, Austria, 1976.

2   M. Grenon, On Fossil Fuel Reserves and Resources. RM-78-35. International Institute for Applied Systems Analysis, Laxenburg, Austria, 1978.

3   Lewin and Associates, Inc., The Potential and Economics of Enhanced Oil Recovery, Washington, D.C., April 1976.

4   V. Pominov, Methods for Increasing the Recovery of Liquid and Gaseous Hydro-carbons from Underground Deposits. Report to the United Nations Economic and Social Council. Economic Commission for Europe, ECE/AC.3/R.4, Geneva, February 1977.

5   Shell UK Ltd., private communication.

6   Amoco U.K., private communication.

7   Mobil Producing North Sea Ltd., private communication.

8   Hamilton Brothers Oil Co., private communication.

9   Chevron Petroleum Co. Ltd., private communication.

10   Occidental Petroleum U.K. Ltd., private communication.

11   BNOC, private communication.

12   U.K. Offshore Operators Association, private communication.

13   United Kingdom Department of Energy, private communication.

14   British Petroleum Development Ltd., private communication.

15   ELF-Aquitaine, private communication.

16   Bredero-Price B.V., private communication.

17   Unocal Exploration and Production Co. U.K. Ltd., private communication.

18   Texaco, private communication.

19   Conoco, private communication.

20   Phillips Petroleum Exploration U.K. Ltd., private communication.

21   Marathon Oil North Sea (G.B.) Ltd., private communication.

22   C.A. Brown, Status Report on the North Sea Development Drilling Market. Riggs National Bank, Washington, D.C., August 1977.

23   Western Geophysical Ltd., private communication.

24   P. Parker, C. Clement, and R. Beirute, Today's oil-well cements offer operators a variety of choices. Oil and Gas Journal, February 21, 1977, p. 62.

25   J.R. Massey, Installation of large rotating equipment systems takes care. Oil and Gas Journal, February 21, 1977, p. 80.

26   D.F. Hemming, Energy Requirements of North Sea Oil Production. Research Report No. ERG 010, Open University, December 1975.

27   E. Macleod, Process Analysis on BP Forties Field. Energy Study Unit, University of Strathclyde, May 1976.

28   Manpower, Materials, and Capital Costs for Energy-Related Facilities. Bechtel Corporation, April 1976, pp. 262–413.

29   Platform report: Brent A jacket prepared for float-out. Ocean Industry, May 1976, p. 94.

30   The Brent Field. Shell U.K. Ltd., 1976.

31   Benefits of North Sea Oil. The Oil Development Council for Scotland, 1977.

32   A. Cottrill, Delicate operator on Beryl. Offshore Engineer, August 1976.

33   A. Stein, Institute for Steel Construction, Technical University of Vienna, private communication.

34   Project Ninian. Chevron Petroleum (U.K.) Ltd.

35   Engineering Handbook of Conversion Factors. GE-NATCO Combustion Engineering, Inc., P.O. Box 1710, Tulsa, Oklahoma 74101, 1974.

36   B.P. Forties Field Facts and Figures. Dix & Motive Press, London.

37   Forties: The Story of Britain's First Major Oilfield. Whitton Print Service Ltd., British Petroleum Co. Ltd., 1976.

38   Statistical Abstract of the U.S. United States Department of Commerce, Bureau of the Census, 1976, pp. 754–792.

39   R.J. Peckham, Joint Research Centre, Commission of the European Communities, Ispra, Italy, 1978, unpublished work.

40   A. Verbraeck, The Energy Accounting of Materials, Products, Processes, and Services. Presented at the 9th International TND Conference (co-sponsored by VNCI and FME), Rotterdam, February 26 and 27, 1976.

BIBLIOGRAPHY

The bibliography is divided into four sections. The first provides a general survey of the available literature, and the entries are arranged in alphabetical order of author. The second section reviews the more important unsigned articles relating to the North Sea which have appeared in four of the leading oil and gas trade periodicals. The third section lists several relevant HMSO publications, and the final section includes miscellaneous reports from the oil companies and elsewhere.

GENERAL SURVEY

Aalund, L.R. (1979). Guide to world crudes. North Sea crudes are examined. Oil and Gas Journal, November 26, 1979, pp. 49–113.

Asheim, H.A., Podio, A.L., and Knapp, R.M. (1980). Costs correlated for North Sea platforms. Oil and Gas Journal, May 5, 1980, pp. 205, 206, 208, 213, 214, 216.

Beirute, R. (1977). Cementing calculations essential part of design stage of project. Oil and Gas Journal, May 9, 1977, pp. 58–61.

Bilderbeck, M. (1980). Innovations help develop marginal North Sea field. Oil and Gas Journal, June 2, 1980, pp. 82, 87, 88, 90.

Brown, C.A. (1976). Forecast of North Sea development well drilling. Ocean Industry, May 1976, pp. 52, 53, 55.

Bühring, W.A. (1975). A model of Environmental Impacts from Electrical Generation in Wisconsin. University of Wisconsin-Madison, Department of Nuclear Engineering.

Charles, K.B. (1976). Symposium on Offshore Drilling Rigs. The Royal Institution of Naval Architects.

Clement. C. (1977). Flow charts remove the guesswork from slurry design. Oil and Gas Journal, March 28, 1977, pp. 143–150.

Clement, C. and Parker, P. (1977). Slurry and pumping guidelines smooth casing-cementing jobs. Oil and Gas Journal, April 11, 1977, pp. 54–58.

Clement, C. and Parker, P. (1977). Auxiliary cementing materials contribute to successful jobs. Oil and Gas Journal, May 23, 1977, pp. 80–84.

Clement, C. and Parker, P. (1977). Additives tailor cement to individual wells. Oil and Gas Journal, March 14, 1977, pp. 55–58.

Collins, B. (1975). U.K. to press drive for 51% of North Sea fields. Oil and Gas Journal, November 24, 1975, pp. 17, 18, 20.

Collins, B. (1976). Billions spent to make oil flow from North Sea. Oil and Gas Journal, June 28, 1976, pp. 87–89, 91–95.

Cottrill, A. (1979). Murchison – the year of the big launch. Offshore Engineer, September 1979, pp. 189–193.

Cranfield, J. and Buckmon, D. (1979). U.K.: the emphasis is on production. World Oil, August 15, 1979, pp. 129, 130, 132, 134, 136, 138, 140, 142.

Cranfield, J. (1979). Subsea system ready for hookup at Murchison field. Ocean Industry, April 1979, pp. 166, 168, 170, 172.

Daniels, B.E. (1977). Slurry design, transport velocity keys to pipelining solids. Oil and Gas Journal, May 16, 1977, pp. 167, 168.

Dean, F.E. (1975). Onshore Development of the Frigg Gas Field. British Gas Corporation, May 1975.

Enright, R.J. (1975). Steel or concrete platforms for the North Sea – or neither? Oil and Gas Journal, June 30, 1975, pp. 115, 116, 118, 121.

Enright, R.J. (1975), The North Sea at last beginning to give up its oil. Oil and Gas Journal, June 30, 1975, pp. 82–88, 91, 92, 94.

Ewing, R.C. (1974). Work starts on North Sea's deepest pipeline. Oil and Gas Journal, June 24, 1974, pp. 126–130.

Ewing, R.C. (1975). New vessels extend pipe-laying limits. Oil and Gas Journal, May 5, 1975, pp. 188–190, 192, 194, 197, 199, 200, 204, 207.

Ewing, R.C. (1976). Marine-pipeline frontiers disappear. Oil and Gas Journal, January 12, 1976, pp. 65–72.

Ewing, R.C. (1977). Subsea pipeliners' know-how gets the job done. Oil and Gas Journal, January 3, 1977, pp. 47–52.

Fowler, C. (1974). The Geology of the Montrose Field. Amoco (UK) Exploration Co., London.

Gillen, W. (1976). U.K. North Sea potential still growing. World Oil, August 15, 1976, pp. 90–96.

Gordon, H.W., Jr. (1975). Concepts refined for deepwater lines. Oil and Gas Journal, September 1, 1975, pp. 120–125.

Gordy, C.J. and Thomas, A.W. (1975). Hamilton's Argyll Semi-submersible/Production-Riser Concept. American Institute of Mining, Metallurgical, and Petroleum Engineers, Inc.

Gray, S. (1974). Oil from troubled waters: what's next for North Sea. World Oil, January 1974, pp. 100–108.

Heaney, J. (1973). In the North Sea Shell outlines Brent, Auk production plans. World Oil, June 1973, pp. 53, 56, 57.

Hodson, G.M. (1975). New log data give better North Sea well completions. World Oil, September 1975, pp. 60–65.

Irish, J. (1978). Murchison gives Conoco team chance for subsea system innovations. Offshore Engineer. September 1978, pp. 28–31.

Kash, D.E., White, I.L., Bergey, K.H., et al. (1973). Energy Under the Oceans. University of Oklahoma Press, pp. 29–31.

Kennedy, J.L. (1974). Billion-dollar-plus Forties. Oil and Gas Journal, June 3, 1974, pp. 106–109.

Kennedy, J.L. (1975). Production scheme uses converted semi-production riser. Oil and Gas Journal, June 30, 1975, pp. 79–81.

Kennedy, J.L. (1977). Offshore water-injection system at Dubai is expanded. Oil and Gas Journal, May 30, 1977, pp. 85–90.

Kennedy, J.L. (1975). New types of gravity platforms near completion. Oil and Gas Journal, May 5, 1975, pp. 210, 212, 217, 218, 220.

Knox, P.L. (1976). Social well-being and North Sea oil: an application of subjective social indicators. Regional Studies, Vol. 10, pp. 423–432.

Koch, R.D. (1976). Forties drilling involves high angles, Gumbo. Oil and Gas Journal, December 13, 1976, pp. 70–77.

Lapillone, B. and Grübler, A. (1976). WELMM Analysis of Nuclear: Resource Requirements for the Operation and Construction of Nuclear Related Facilities.

Larsen, H.L., Kuzma, J.H., and Pellegrino, V.L. (1977). Energy conservation trims costs. Oil and Gas Journal, April 11, 1977, pp. 65, 66, 71–74.

Lighthill, J. (1977). Multiple sea use. Interdisciplinary Science Reviews, Vol. 2, No. 1, pp. 27–35.

Linder, J.T. and Hartley, G. (1979). North Sea's deepest catenary anchor leg mooring system. Ocean Industry, October 1979, pp. 133, 135, 136.

Long, J. (1975). North Sea venture. The Lamp, Vol. 57, No. 4, (Winter 1975), pp. 7–25.

Lund, S. (1976). Statfjord-to-Norway pipeline. Oil and Gas Journal, July 26, 1976, pp. 115–121.

Massad, A.H. (1976). Production to start from subsea; wellhead completion in Beryl field. Oil and Gas Journal, June 28, 1976, pp. 100–102, 107, 108, 113, 114.

Matheny, S., Jr., (1980). Tanker to handle and store Fulmar oil. Oil and Gas Journal, May 5, 1980, pp. 226, 229, 230, 234.

O'Brien, T.B. (1976). Drilling costs: a current appraisal of a major problem. World Oil, October 1976, pp. 75–78.

Parker, P., Clement, C., and Beirute, R.M. (1977). Today's oil-well cements offer operators a variety of choices. Oil and Gas Journal, February 21, 1977, pp. 59–64.

Parker, P. (1977). Speciality cements can solve problems. Oil and Gas Journal, February 28, 1977, pp. 128–131.

Primm, L.A. (1977). After a few years' use, collars with ER grooves had fewer connection failures. World Oil, January 1977, pp. 87–89.

Ridgway, G. (1979). Beatrice–BNOC bustles blithely. Offshore Engineer, September 1979, p. 136.

Sanderson, B.M. (1976). Brent field gas facilities under way. Oil and Gas Journal, September 6, 1976, pp. 123–126.

Seaton, E. (1976). Brent field nears first oil delivery. Oil and Gas Journal, January 26, 1976, pp. 125–129.

Shaub, D.P. (1976). Offshore Pipeline Report: Line from Ekofisk to Emden nearly completed. Oil and Gas Journal, January 12, 1976, pp. 78–85.

Thompson, R.M. (1976). European pipeliners try new coatings. Oil and Gas Journal, July 5, 1976, pp. 92, 93, 96.

Trainor, R.W., Scott, J.R., and Cairns, W.J. (1976). Design and construction of a marine terminal for North Sea oil in Orkney, Scotland. Offshore Technology Conference. Dallas, Texas, 1976.

Van Hussen, G. (1976). Hammer is designed for deepwater pile driving. Oil and Gas Journal, October 18, 1976, pp. 67–69.

Vielvoye, R. (1980). North Sea report: North Sea oil flow tops 2 million b/d. Oil and Gas Journal, June 2, 1980, pp. 75–81.

Vielvoye, R. (1980). North Sea report: Shell sees good potential for enhanced recovery. Oil and Gas Journal, June 2, 1980, pp. 112, 117.

Voss, J.M. (1977). Energy to year 2000: Caltex Corp. takes a long look ahead. World Oil, May 1977, pp. 68–78.

Wilson, G.E. (1976). How to drill a useable hole. World Oil, October 1976, pp. 99–102.

UNSIGNED ARTICLES FOR OIL- AND GAS-INDUSTRY PERIODICALS

Softer participation policy pays off in U.K. North Sea. Oil and Gas Journal, June 28, 1976, pp. 59–61, 64, 72.

World crude-price picture foggier still. Oil and Gas Journal, January 3, 1977, p. 34.

CIA Director denies report political. Oil and Gas Journal, May 2, 1977, pp. 117, 118.

Development pace frenzied off U.K. Oil and Gas Journal, August 28, 1978, pp. 75, 76, 89, 90.

Smaller fields eyed off the U.K. Oil and Gas Journal, June 4, 1979, pp. 87, 92–94, 99, 102, 107, 108.

Higher oil prices spark action in the North Sea. Oil and Gas Journal, March 10, 1980, pp. 43–47.

How some North Sea costs have jumped. Oil and Gas Journal, June 30, 1975, pp. 74, 75.

The big, fast crane for the big, tough jobs. Oil and Gas Journal, April 25, 1977, p. 130.

Esso, Shell to build $70 million barge for North Sea pipe laying. Oil and Gas Journal, May 20, 1974, p. 57.

Dragon joins offshore fleet. Oil and Gas Journal, March 7, 1977, p. 121.

Specify proper wellhead material. Oil and Gas Journal, January 24, 1977, pp. 63–66.

Satellite communication set for Gulf platform. Oil and Gas Journal, July 22, 1974, pp. 18, 19.

Underground gas storage tops 6 trillion. Oil and Gas Journal, July 1, 1974, p. 33.

Offshore report: packaged water-injection plant aimed at offshore use. Oil and Gas Journal, May 2, 1977, pp. 191, 192, 195, 196.

North Sea report: Ekofisk-to-Emden gas line international affair. Oil and Gas Journal, June 3, 1974, p. 110.

Pipeline pulls completed in the Orkneys. Oil and Gas Journal, May 3, 1976, pp. 188, 193, 194.

Barge lays 2.34 miles of pipeline in 1 day. Oil and Gas Journal, October 11, 1976, pp. 114, 119.

Tenneco asks approval for LNG import line. Oil and Gas Journal, December 27, 1976, pp. 78, 79.